Convergence of Blockchain, AI and IoT

Convergence of Blockchain, AI and IoT: A Digital Platform discusses the convergence of three powerful technologies that play into the digital revolution and blur the lines between biological, digital, and physical objects. This book covers novel algorithms, solutions for addressing issues in applications, security, authentication, and privacy.

- Discusses innovative technological upgradation and significant challenges in the current era
- Gives an overview of clinical scientific research that enables smart diagnosis through artificial intelligence
- Provides an insight into how disruptive technology enabled with the self-running devices and protection mechanism is involved in an augmented reality with blockchain mechanism
- Talks about neural science being capable of enhancing deep brain waves to predict an overall improvement in human thoughts and behaviours
- Covers the digital currency mechanism in detail
- Enhances the knowledge of readers about smart contract and ledger mechanism with artificial intelligence and blockchain mechanism

Targeted audiences range from those interested in the technical revolution of blockchain, big data and the Internet of Things, to research scholars and the professional market.

Convergence of Blockchain, AI and IoT
A Digital Platform

B. Balamurugan, T. Poongodi, M. R. Manu,
S. Karthikeyan and Yogesh Sharma

CRC Press
Taylor & Francis Group
Boca Raton London New York

CRC Press is an imprint of the
Taylor & Francis Group, an **informa** business

First edition published 2023
by CRC Press
6000 Broken Sound Parkway NW, Suite 300, Boca Raton, FL 33487-2742

and by CRC Press
4 Park Square, Milton Park, Abingdon, Oxon, OX14 4RN

CRC Press is an imprint of Taylor & Francis Group, LLC

© 2023 B. Balamurugan, T. Poongodi, M. R. Manu, S. Karthikeyan and Yogesh Sharma

Library of Congress Cataloging-in-Publication Data
Names: Balusamy, Balamurugan, author. | Poongodi, T., author. |
Manu M. R. (Manu Ramachandran), author. | S., Karthikeyan, author. |
Sharma, Yogesh (Professor of computer science and engineering), author.
Title: Convergence of blockchain, AI and IoT : a digital platform /
B Balamurugan, T Poongodi, Manu M R, Karthikeyan S, Yogesh Sharma.
Description: First edition. | Boca Raton : Chapman & Hall/CRC Press, 2023. |
Includes bibliographical references and index.
Identifiers: LCCN 2022017673 (print) | LCCN 2022017674 (ebook) |
ISBN 9780367495305 (hardback) | ISBN 9780367495343 (paperback) |
ISBN 9781003046462 (ebook)
Subjects: LCSH: Blockchains (Databases) | Internet of things. | Artificial intelligence.
Classification: LCC QA76.9.B56 B25 2023 (print) |
LCC QA76.9.B56 (ebook) | DDC 005.74–dc23/eng/20220726
LC record available at https://lccn.loc.gov/2022017673
LC ebook record available at https://lccn.loc.gov/2022017674

ISBN: 9780367495305 (hbk)
ISBN: 9780367495343 (pbk)
ISBN: 9781003046462 (ebk)

DOI: 10.1201/9781003046462

Typeset in Palatino
by Newgen Publishing UK

Contents

Preface

The world is growing with technological and scientific developments which provide intense benefits in human quality of life and economic growth. The availability and manipulation of data is a crucial area. The three main aspects in data science, blockchain, IoT and artificial intelligence, are combined with with different aspects which shows some similarities when we focus more deeply. *Convergence of Blockchain, AI and IoT: Digital Platform* discusses a transformation in the digital world to a new revolution in the computing world.

At its core, the optimization of the Internet of Things with its resilience and reliability mechanisms is discussed in this book. The deep brain mechanism involved in this book discusses the next-generation innovation in industrial aspects of the blockchain mechanism. The future enhancements with the convergence of these three technologies will enhance economic growth with digital currency and clinical diagnosis. This book also enhances strategic technological trends through spectrum computing and smart contract techniques. The swarm intelligent mechanism described in this book provides a diversion to artificial intelligence towards blockchain. The key concepts of this book will provide a futuristic overview towards the reader about the new technologies and their combination with realistic nature in a wider sense in this digital world.

This book is categorized into seven general areas:

1: Optimization of the IoT through Artificial Intelligence
2: Fundamentals of the IoT, AI and Blockchain
3: Transformation of Artificial Intelligence towards the IoT
4: Transformation of Artificial Intelligence towards Blockchain
5: Technological Transformation of the IoT towards Blockchain
6: Futuristic approach to the IoT, AI and Blockchain
7: Revolutionary Aspects in the Digital World

Author Biographies

Dr. B. Balamurugan completed his Ph.D. at VIT University, Vellore and currently works as a Professor in Galgotias University, Greater Noida, Uttar Pradesh. He has 15 years of teaching experience in the field of computer science. His areas of interest lie in the field of the Internet of Things, big data and networking. He has published more than 100 international journals papers and contributed numerous book chapters.

Dr. T. Poongodi works as an Associate Professor, in the School of Computing Science and Engineering, Galgotias University, Delhi—NCR, India. She has completed her Ph.D in Information Technology (Information and Communication Engineering) from Anna University, Tamil Nadu, India. Her areas of research interests include big data, wireless ad-hoc network, Internet of Things, network security and blockchain technology. She has published more than 50 papers in various international journals, national/international conferences, and book chapters published by Springer, Elsevier, Wiley, De-Gruyter, CRC Press, and IGI Global, and edited books published by CRC, IET, Wiley, Springer, and Apple Academic Press.

Mr. M. R. Manu currently works as a Faculty in the Ministry of Education, Abudabi, UAE. He worked as an Assistant Professor in the School of Computing Science and Engineering, Galgotias University, NCR Delhi, India. He has completed an ME in Computer Science and Engineering from Anna University Taramani Campus, Tamil Nadu, India and currently is pursuing a Ph.D. in Computer Science and Engineering from Galgotias University NCR Delhi, India. His areas of interest are big data, networks and network security. He has undertaken a number of research projects in networks specialization and published 20 papers in various international and national journals and published four patents in the fields of artificial intelligence and blockchain. He is currently writing a monograph and book chapters for CRC Press, Springer, and Elsevier publishers.

Mr. S. Karthikeyan is currently working as an Assistant Professor in the Department of Computer Science & Engineering (Specialization) School of Engineering & Technology, Jain University, He has worked as an Assistant Professor in the School of Computing Science and Engineering, Galgotias University, NCR Delhi, India. He has completed an ME in Computer Science and Engineering from Anna University, Tamil Nadu, India, and currently is pursuing a Ph.D. in Computer Science and Engineering from Galgotias University NCR Delhi, India. His areas of interest are cloud computing and IoT security. He has undertaken a number of research projects and published book chapters and papers in various international journals and books. He is currently writing monograph and book chapters for CRC Press, Springer, and Elsevier publishers.

Mr. Yogesh Sharma works as an Assistant Professor in the Department of Computer Science and Engineering in Maharaja Agrasen Institute of Technology, Delhi, India. He has completed an ME in Computer Technology and Application at Delhi Technological University (formerly Delhi College of Engineering), Delhi, India, and currently is pursuing a Ph.D. in Computer Science and Engineering from Galgotias University NCR Delhi, India. His interests lie in the fields of big data, data mining, Network security and blockchain. He has published 10 papers in various international and national journals (Scopus index). He has also gained two patents in the areas of digital modulation and blockchain.

Introduction

The digital revolution is characterized by the convergence of technologies which are rapidly advancing the fourth industrial revolution and blurring the lines between physical, digital and biological objects. The fourth revolution is evolving at an exponential rate which cannot be compared with any previous technologies. AI and the IoT employ interactions and operations in various fields such as home appliances, autonomous vehicles, nanotechnology, robotics, cognitive systems, self-driving cars and wearable devices. The potential of blockchain technology is realized in many sectors nowadays as security plays a vital role everywhere. There has been a tremendous increase in the usage of AI and IoT technologies by various companies. AI has huge potential to identify the patterns and anomalies in the data generated by IoT sensors. The accuracy of operational predictions using AI technologies is greater as compared to threshold-based monitoring systems. IoT and connected systems drive AI as intelligent automation, making sense of data generated from sensor devices in decision-making processes. Blockchain plays a significant role in providing security during data-handling operations. Blockchain defines how trusted transactions can be carried out and it addresses the solution for vulnerability problems faced by the internet. Blockchain solves the security fault line among AI and IoT where most of the IoT devices are connected to each other through public networks. Linear and permanent indexed records are maintained in blockchain to address the vulnerability issues. Many applications and concepts are already in practice that overlap with these technologies with promising results. Gaining control of devices and records is difficult in the blockchain system in such a way that blocks are maintained and guarded. IoT devices share information via public networks, which introduces vulnerability and risks which are increased if AI is also involved. Moreover, the blockchain system has robust security implementations that are affordable, scalable, secure and verifiable for the platform. The peer-to-peer model is a competent solution for the effective communication in a centralized client/server paradigm. Blockchain ensures security by using a distributed ledger shared among nodes in the network for transactions. Transactions are verified using cryptographic techniques to authenticate and identify the nodes, hence there is no role for any central authority. Nowadays, smart IoT medical devices are guided by AI to make lifesaving decisions using biometric data. In smart vehicles, IoT sensors are fixed in the car to give alert if any fault occurs in any part of the car. In such a case, AI assists the sensor in detecting faults with the help of data generated by IoT devices. In addition, if blockchain is incorporated then the situation again changes. Once the sensor detects a fault then the insurance

DOI: 10.1201/9781003046462-1

claim will be automatically credited to the user's account. In fact, the convergence of blockchain, AI and the IoT will revolutionize the insurance industry. Consider that self-driving trucks are designed with AI technologies to dispatch goods to distribution centres. Self-driving cars should be directed to a charging station for automatic charging. A smart contract framework enables the truck to be charged in the charging station after proper authentication and authorization. The ledger issued to record the transaction in the smart contract makes the system more secure, which prevents tampering. Goods can be delivered to customers with IoT devices employed and monitored by retail companies. AI algorithms assess on-site safety management to examine the heat stress levels of workers using IoT sensor devices to measure data such as humidity, temperature, etc. This scenario would be complete if workers are insured and the blockchain system is implemented for assuring security. An AI algorithm detects the heat stress of workers and ensures worker safety, while the blockchain ensures prompt insurance. All these combined technologies can leverage the combined effectiveness and suggest a way for a platform where data can be generated, processed and secured by making use of the IoT system, AI algorithm and blockchain technology.

1

An Introduction to IoT Technologies

The Internet of Things (IoT) is a rapidly emerging paradigm in which physical or virtual objects equipped with sensors, actuators, processors and transceivers are connected with each other to enable communication among themselves. Some of the most significant IoT technologies are highlighted by reviewing state-of-the-art techniques, protocols and applications to bring about a striking difference in day-to-day life. This chapter is very inclusive in its coverage and exhaustively spans the major IoT technologies from sensors to applications. Artificial intelligence (AI) is a constantly and actively growing technology focused on intelligent agents which observe the environment in order to take appropriate actions. In the modern digitized world, AI machines perform creative and intellectual functions to uncover solutions by solving problems independently. Blockchains are tamper-resistant digital ledgers that record transactions in a distributed manner without the involvement of any central authorities and repositories. A community of users can record their transactions in a shared ledger; no transaction can be modified in the blockchain network once it has been published. The chapter provides an overview of blockchain technology that assists readers to understand how it works.

1.1 An Introduction to the Internet of Things in a Real-World Scenario

The IoT is a widely emerging paradigm in which physical or virtual objects equipped with sensors, actuators, transceivers and processors enable communication among each other in order to provide a meaningful service to human life, specifically for elderly and differently abled. Recently, the Internet has become considered as ubiquitous since it reaches every corner of the world, impacting human life in incredible ways. Moreover, pervasive connectivity facilitates a number of appliances to be connected with the web. The Internet of Things is defined as it enables interaction between the physical and digital environments. Also, the digital world is connected to the physical

DOI: 10.1201/9781003046462-2

world using a variety of sensors and actuators. The Internet of Things is also defined as a paradigm that consists of computing capabilities with several conceivable objects. Such kinds of capabilities are ease to identify and change the state of an object whenever required. In general, the Internet of Things implies that all kinds of appliances and devices are connected to a network, and are collaboratively utilized to solve complex tasks that necessitate a high degree of intelligence.

Sensors and actuators play a significant role in enabling communication between the physical and digital worlds. The data gathered by sensors should be maintained and processed in an intellectual way to obtain meaningful inferences from it. A microwave oven or a mobile phone can be considered as a sensor since input data can be obtained about the surrounding environment. An actuator is mainly utilized to observe changes in the environment, for example, the role of the temperature controller in an air conditioner.

The IoT has been made possible by recent advancements in smart sensors, RFID, communication technologies, networking systems, and Internet protocols (IPs). Also, the elementary concept is that smart sensors can function together without human intervention to create several applications. Moreover, the recent revolution in Internet, smartphone, and machine-to-machine (M2M) has paved the way for using the IoT system to a greater extent. The IoT is anticipated to bridge various technologies by integrating physical objects in the forthcoming years which support intelligent decision-making in different applications. The IoT is being realized with an ever-increasing number of physical objects linked to the Internet at an exponential rate. HVAC (heating, ventilation and air conditioning) monitoring systems are examples of smart homes that connect smart objects. There are a variety of other areas and contexts in which the IoT can make a significant difference and enhance human life styles. Transportation, industrial automation, healthcare and emergency responses to sudden disasters where decision-making by humans is challenging are all examples of these applications [1].

Intelligent technologies have been developed across a variety of areas. Although not all of these technologies are presently available, preliminary research suggests that the IoT has the potential to enhance the quality of life in all communities. Intelligent applications have been built across a wide range of domains. Moreover, there are a few applications that aren't yet operational. Health monitoring, home automation, environment safety, fitness tracking, industrial sectors and smart cities are some examples of IoT applications [2].

1.1.1 Smart Home

Because of two factors, smart homes are becoming more common nowadays. The first factor is that sensor and actuator systems, as well as the wireless sensor network (WSN), have advanced significantly. The second factor is that people nowadays have faith in technology to provide the solutions to enrich their quality of life and provide home protection. Various sensors can be fixed in smart homes in order to provide several automated services to the customer. They assist in automating everyday activities and the maintenance of a schedule for people who are prone to forgetfulness. Furthermore, they contribute to energy efficiency by automatically shutting off electronic devices and lights. For this, normally, motion sensors are used.

Motion sensors may also be exploited for surveillance purposes. For instance, MayHome is a project that affords an intelligent agent which employs several prediction algorithms to perform tasks automatically in response to user-triggered events according to the residents' routines. The series of events in a home is predicted using prediction algorithms. Also, the sequence matching algorithm keeps track of event sequences and their frequencies. Factors such as length and frequency are then used to create a forecast. Markov models and compression-based prediction techniques are two other algorithms which can be used for similar applications.

Sensors are widely used with adequate context awareness in smart homes in order to reduce electricity usage. These sensors gather information from the surrounding environment (e.g., humidity, light, gas, temperature, pressure, etc.). Also, the data from various sensors are provided as input into a context aggregator, which later sends the information to the context-aware service engine. This engine then selects resources by considering the current situation. When the humidity level increases, for instance, an application will automatically switch on the air conditioner. It can also switch off all the lights if there is a gas leak. For aged people and differently abled persons, smart home systems are extremely advantageous. Their well-being is tracked, and in the case of an emergency, relatives are notified immediately.

Pressure sensors are installed into the floors to monitor a person's movements in the smart home and to detect whether he or she has fallen. CCTV cameras can be used in smart homes to capture significant moments. They can then be used to extract features in order to create an overall picture of occurrences. Moreover, the fall detection applications, in particular, are helpful in detecting when elderly people have fallen or slipped. Human body postures can be analyzed using computer vision techniques. Less expensive infrared sensor technology can provide information on a target object's position, scale and velocity. It analyzes motion patterns to detect the dynamics of a fall, as well as inactivity, and compares it to previous activity. For different kinds of falls, neural networks are used, and the sample data are provided to the machine. There are also a number of smartphone-based apps that can detect a fall using data from a gyroscope and accelerometer.

When it comes to smart home applications, there are many problems and issues that remain. The most important is privacy and security, since data are recorded regarding the events that take place in the home. An intruder can attack the system and cause it to act maliciously if the system's trustworthiness and security are not assured. In the case that any anomalies are observed, smart home systems are expected to alert the owners. AI and machine learning algorithms can be used for these kinds of activities, and researchers are already working on it. Due to the absence of a system administrator to control the system, reliability is also considered to be a major issue.

1.1.2   Smart Cities

Smart transportation systems use intelligent information-processing systems with different sensors to control everyday traffic in cities. Intelligent transportation networks are designed to alleviate traffic congestion, make parking simple and convenient, and prevent accidents by properly directing traffic and detecting drunk drivers. GPS sensors are used to identify the location, accelerometers are used to detect the speed, gyroscopes are used to identify the direction, mainly RFIDs are used for vehicle detection, infrared sensors are used to count the number of passengers and vehicles, and cameras are used for monitoring the traffic and vehicle movement. These are the sensor technologies that control smart transportation of applications. In this domain, there are a variety of applications:

> Traffic surveillance application: A network connects vehicles with a variety of IoT devices, cloud storage including RFID readers, GPS sensors, cameras, etc. Moreover, these instruments are capable of measuring traffic situations in various regions of the city. Also, the custom applications can examine traffic dynamics in order to predict future traffic conditions. Video sequences shot on roads are used in a tracking system for traffic surveillance. The smart sensors, namely, GPS sensors and accelerometers, can also be used to identify traffic congestion. When the user is driving, these applications can recognize the vehicle's movement patterns. Google Maps is already collecting this kind of data, and users are exploiting it to navigate in the highly congested parts of cities.

Smart transportation entails more than just traffic control. It also concerns the protection of passengers in their cars, which was previously mostly in the hands of the vehicle driver. Furthermore, several IoT applications have been created to assist drivers in the aspect of safety. Such applications monitor drivers' driving habits and assist them in driving safely by detecting when they are drowsy or exhausted and assisting them in managing the situation or recommending rest. Technologies such as eye movement detection, face detection and pressure detection are factors which are considered to assess the driver's hand grip on the steering. Also, a smartphone application has been proposed that uses smartphone sensors such as the GPS, gyroscope, accelerometer and camera to estimate the driver's driving attitude. By analyzing sensor data, it can determine whether the driving is safe or risky.

In a smart parking system, parking is absolutely hassle-free in a smart transportation system because one can conveniently search on the Internet to identify which parking lots have vacant spaces. Sensors are used in these parking lots to determine whether the slots are empty or occupied by motor vehicles. Later, this information is submitted to a centralized server. The intelligent traffic light system refers to traffic lights that sense, process and also have communication capabilities to establish a link among connected devices. These lights detect traffic congestion and the amount of traffic flowing in either direction. These data can be processed and then transmitted to nearby traffic lights or a centralized controller for processing. This knowledge can be brought to innovative use. In the case of an emergency, for example, traffic lights can spontaneously provide space to an ambulance. Also, once an intelligent traffic light detects an ambulance arriving, it leaves an opening and alerts nearby lights. Cameras, data processing and communication technology modules are the technologies exploited in these lights. In accident detection systems, with the aid of an acoustic data and accelerometer, a smartphone application has been developed which identifies the occurrence of accidents immediately. It sends this information, as well as the exact location, to the hospital which is nearby. Additional information such as on-site photos, also are frequently communicated. Thus, the responders are informed first about the complete scenario and the medical assistance is provided.

Considering the current levels of water scarcity in various regions of the world, it is crucial to effectively manage the water supply. As a consequence, several cities have been turning to smart cities recently that include installing a large number of meters along storm drains and water lines. The water meters that are fixed on the smart systems can be used to determine how much water comes in and goes out, as well as to locate potential leakages. River water and weather satellite sensors are also used in combination with water metering of smart systems. These can assist in flood forecasting also.

1.1.3 Smart Agriculture

Temperature and humidity are significant environmental factors in the agricultural sector. Farmers use sensors in the region to calculate these factors, and the data can be exploited to improve production efficiency. For instance, automated irrigation is an application which functions based on weather conditions. One of the most common uses of the IoT in agriculture is greenhouse production. Temperature, humidity and soil details, are all variables that are monitored in real time and transmitted to a server for further analysis. After that, the information is utilized significantly to enhance the crop yield and quality. An acetylcholinesterase biosensor is used to identify pesticide residues during crop growth. This information is maintained and analyzed to extract the desired information, including sample size, residue amount, location and time. As a result, the crop quality can be maintained.

A quick response code (QR code) may also be exploited to track the specific part of an agricultural production. Until purchasing, consumers could monitor the QR code and verify the quantity of pesticides on-line with the aid of a centralized database. Today, air pollution is considered to be a major factor as it is affecting the Earth's atmosphere and deteriorating the air quality. Vehicles cause serious impacts on global warming. An IoT device can control the carbon emissions on the roads and also keep track of motor vehicles that pollute the atmosphere excessively. Air emissions can also be measured using electrochemical toxic gas sensors. RFID tags and RFID readers are mounted on both sides of the lane for tracking vehicles. This tool can be used to classify polluting vehicles and assist in taking action against them.

1.1.4 Smart Healthcare

In the healthcare sector, IoT appliances have been proven to be extremely beneficial. Various wearable devices that control an individual's health are being created. Healthcare systems allow elderly people and patients, even with serious illnesses, to lead their life as independently as possible [3]. IoT sensors are currently being exploited to consistently track and record health-related information, as well as send out warnings if any suspicious signs are exposed. If an issue is minor, the IoT application can provide a prescription for the patients. IoT applications could be used to create an electronic health record (EHR), which is a document that contains all of a person's medical information, which the healthcare system maintains. Furthermore, an EHR can be commonly used to monitor allergies, sugar level and changes in blood pressure. Furthermore, stress recognition technology is also very common nowadays and smartphone sensors are generally used to understand them.

An application which is activated on a college student's smartphone could assess the student's stress level. In addition, it can also detect various information such as the locations visited by the student during the daytime, as well as the level of physical activity, sleeping time, interactions and relationships with others (audio/voice calls). A survey could be conducted with students by posing a question to them at random on their smartphones. The stress level and performance in academic activities could be assessed intelligently. Applications in the fitness industry monitor how fit we are based on our daily activity level. Several activities can be detected from smartphone accelerometer data using complex algorithms. Fitness trackers, for example, can be used to track the step count and how much exercise an individual has done [4]. In addition, fitness trackers are wearable devices that can be used to track a person's fitness level. In addition, sensors can be installed on gym equipment to monitor how much exercise has been performed. A smart pad, for instance, will monitor the amount of exercise steps done. This is accomplished by placing sensors on the mat to measure the pressure as well as the contact region shape.

1.1.5 Smart Grid

The smart grid is a contemporary power generation, transmission and distribution infrastructure that is driven by information and communication technology. The principle of smart grids adds intelligence at each phase of the electricity generation, transmission and distribution process, as well as allowing for two-way power flow from the consumer to the supplier and vice versa. Microgrids produce electricity to address the requirements of local premises and then send the excess energy back to the main grid. In the case of any shortfall, microgrids will request energy from the central grid. Consumers who use their own generated energy on occasion (e.g., wind power or solar energy) will benefit from a two-way power flow because the power which is leftover can be transferred back such that it will not be lost. Moreover, the consumer would be charged only for their usage of electricity. Also, the two examples of IoT applications in a smart grid using a smart meter to monitor energy consumption are (i) online transmission line monitoring for disaster prevention and (ii) efficient power utilization in smart homes. During peak load, smart meters analyze the power consumption patterns. After that, the data are transmitted to the centralized server and become accessible to the user. Also, the energy generation process is completely dependent on the consumption patterns. Furthermore, the user could adjust their usage patterns to save money. Smart energy appliances can take advantage of these data and function when prices are low.

1.1.6 Smart Supply Chain

The IoT focuses on improving the real-world activities of enterprise systems making them easier to understand. Using sensor technologies like NFC and RFID, products in the supply chain management could be monitored continuously from the production stage till the distribution stage. For monitoring, real-time data can be recorded and analyzed. RFID tags attached to shipments may also store information about the product's consistency and usability. The IoT is used to suggest an information-sharing framework for a smart supply chain. RFID tags automatically detect a product, and the information network is constructed to send the information, as well as location data, in real time. This framework automates the gathering process and analysis of all data relevant to the supply chain, that could also be used to analyze the past demand and forecast the future demand. Real-time data can be accessed by supply chain components, and these data can be analyzed to gain valuable insights. This would help supply chain networks perform better in this regard.

1.1.7   Social Events and the Entertainment Sector

The smart environment plays a significant role in people's lives. Several applications have been created to monitor the activities performed by humans. Also, sensing capabilities and short-range communication facilities are built into personal devices such as wearables, tablets and mobiles. When there is a common goal, people are able to find and communicate with one another. In a circle sense software application, different types of sensor data are used to detect a person's social activities. It analyzes the generalized patterns related to social activities and the people involved in such kinds of activities, which determines the person's social circle. Various forms of social events, as well as the people who participate in them, are recognized. Also, location sensors are used to calculate where the person is, and Bluetooth is used to scan people who are in the vicinity. Machine learning algorithms are integrated into the framework, and it learns to refine its behavior over time.

Affective computing is a kind of technology that distinguishes, realizes, stimulates and reacts to human emotions. When dealing with real human effects, many aspects are taken into account, including facial expressions, voice, body motions, sleeping patterns and hand movements. These are tested in order to assess the feeling of a particular person. Voice recognition detects the speech of emotional keywords, and acoustic features of speech are used to assess voice quality. Logmusic is an application developed for

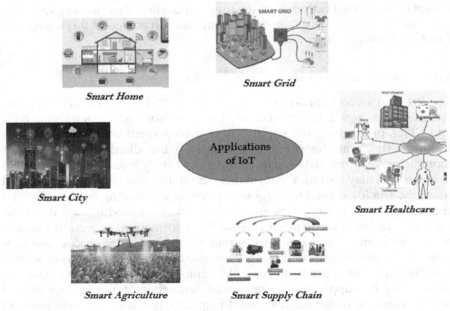

FIGURE 1.1
Applications of the IoT in real-world scenarios.

entertainment purposes that suggests music by focusing on the current situation, such as location, time, weather and temperature. Different applications of the IoT in real-world scenarios are depicted in Figure 1.1.

1.2　A Divergence Approach from Automation toward Artificial Intelligence

Initially, the concept of automation and artificial intelligence alarmed technology experts by the fact that the power and prospects that come with automation and AI would reduce the manpower required, and with that destroys jobs [5]. AI remains a thing of the future, and nobody wants a machine to make decisions and decide the future of any company. For example, what if the machine has gone wrong or some wrong decisions are made, then nobody can be made responsible for that.

The technological upgrading through automation of tasks in industry makes a positive impact on productivity with reduced costs so [6] before going deeper into divergence from automation to artificial intelligence we need to understand what automation is.

1.2.1　About Automation

Automation is the use of electronics and computer-controlled devices to assume control of processes; automation makes things work automatically, i.e., by themselves with little or no direct human control. The aim of automation is to boost efficiency and reliability. In many cases however, automation replaces labor. In fact, economists today fear that new technology will eventually put hundreds of millions of people in many manufacturing plants out of work worldwide. Today robotic assembly lines are progressively carrying out functions that humans used to do. Automation encompasses many key elements, systems and job functions. In virtually all industries automation is prevalent, especially in manufacturing and transportation facility operations and utilities, additionally national defense systems are becoming increasingly automated. Automation today exists in all functions within industry including integration, installation, procurement, maintenance and even marketing and sales. Bill Gates has often expressed concerns regarding artificial intelligence and the automation that comes with it. Elon Musk has expressed similar concerns about what will happen to humans as artificial intelligence becomes more sophisticated and smarter. The late professor Hawking said it would take off on its own and redesign itself at an ever-increasing rate, while humans, who are limited by slow biological evolution, would be unable to compete and would be superseded. Many economists claim that we should not fear automation and argue that it creates new well-paying jobs. However, won't we reach a point one day when robots and computers can do everything better and faster than humans? If we reach that point what happens to us, what will our role be in a fully automated world.

1.2.2   Building Blocks of Artificial Intelligence

There are in all few building blocks of AI that are necessary in the process of designing and assembling of any AI system. Any AI system that is created always possesses the basic functionality and building blocks but the system is often modified by companies in order to customize the system according to their specific needs. A simple AI system could be made by using only one building block, but as time passes the system evolves to combine more blocks in the system [7]. These building blocks are discussed below.

1.2.2.1   *Knowledge Engineering*

Knowledge engineering (KE) refers to all technical, scientific and social aspects involved in building, maintaining and using knowledge-based systems [8]. One of the first examples of an expert system was Meissen, an application to perform medical diagnoses. In the Meissen example the domain experts were medical doctors and the knowledge represented was their expertise and diagnosis. Expert systems were first developed in artificial intelligence laboratories as an attempt to understand complex human decision-making based on positive results from these initial prototypes [9]. The technology was adopted by the US business community and later worldwide in the 1980s. The Stanford heuristic programming projects were led by Edward Feigenbaum, who was one of the leaders in defining and developing the first expert systems. In the earliest days of expert systems there was little or no formal process for the creation of the software. Researchers just sat down with domain experts and started programming, often developing the required tools, for example, inference engines, at the same time as the applications themselves. As expert systems moved from academic prototypes to deployment in business systems it was realized that a methodology was required to bring about predictability and control to the process of building the software [10]. There were essentially two approaches that were attempted, the first was to use conventional software development methodologies and the second was to develop special methodologies tuned to the requirements of building expert systems. Many of the early expert systems were developed by large consulting and system integration firms, such as Anderson consulting. These firms already had well-tested conventional waterfall methodologies, for example, the slash and burn method, for Anderson that they trained all their staff in and that were virtually always used to develop software for their clients. One trend in early expert systems development was to simply apply these waterfall methods to expert systems development. Another issue with using conventional methods to develop expert systems was that due to the unprecedented nature of expert systems they were one of the first applications to adopt rapid application development methods that featured iteration and prototyping instead of detailed analysis and design. In the 1980s few conventional software methods supported this type of approach. The final issue with using conventional methods to develop expert systems was a need for knowledge acquisition. Knowledge acquisition refers to the process of gathering expert knowledge and capturing it in the form of rules and ontology [11]. Knowledge acquisition has special requirements beyond the conventional specification process used to capture most business requirements. These issues led to the second approach to knowledge engineering, which is the development of custom methodologies specifically designed to build expert systems. One of the first and most popular of these methodologies of custom design for expert systems was knowledge acquisition and documentation structuring.

1.2.2.2 Robotics Automation

Robotic process automation (RPA) refers to automating of white-collar work. Therefore, the word robot basically means that we are programming a computer, an algorithm, to do things that previously humans did; especially some of the rule-based and more structured processes in companies we be automated [12]. So, let's think about a call center for example, where a call center agent handles a complaint call , they would open a certain window, look up certain documents, trace something else, maybe put a few numbers into different fields and calculate the result. All of this can be automated and, in the past, we used robotic process automation and had to basically program this in so a human had to watch what the process was, document the process and then write it down and program a robot to do it. Nowadays, we have robotic process automation which is enabled by artificial intelligence and machine learning, and basically means that machines can simply watch us and see what we do and then automatically learn from this and suggest amendments and improve our processes and automate certain parts of the process [13]. So just think about this intelligent software layer in a call center that watches what is taking place over a month and then over time learning it so that when someone rings in with a complaint it will automatically open the correct window, automatically make some of those calculations, automatically pre-fill some of the forms and so on. Nowadays things are as in the above statements, and in this busy world for a particular job an employee can receive mail about a job or for consulting in some engagement in a different manner. Even email conversations are very similar in their own words, for example, where you say "Okay give me some more details on this," then there could be some negotiation on price. Now, all of this could be automated if there were a software layer that was intelligent, which would watch me for a month or so and then learn and pre-populate some of these emails or even run them automatically. Therefore, Gartner, an IT and consulting company that does lots of research on technology, predicted that 85 percent of all large companies will have some sort of robotic process automation in operation by 2020 [14]. This looks very real. The American insurance company American Fidelity basically figured out that every hour they spend on robotic process automation will save them 10 hours in time afterwards, giving huge benefits. All of these can be automated using robotic process automation and increasingly without even programming, but simply having an artificial intelligence-infused RPA tool.

1.2.2.3 *Speech Recognition*

The goal of speech recognition is to generate methodologies and technologies that enable the recognition and also the translation of spoken language into text [15]. The perfect example for this can be found in a video, where if a viewer wishes to read the subtitles on the video, by clicking on the subtitles button we will see that an algorithm is recognizing the words and transforming them into text that can be read. Similar technologies are used in other applications such as Google Translate, Apple's Siri or Amazon's Alexa. Speech recognition is often associated with speech to text, which means that once the computer recognizes words it writes them down in the form of text. Sometimes the computer is not seen to be transforming speech into text but this doesn't mean that is not happening. Actually, behind the scenes most natural language technologies work on texts and not on voices. In fact, when you ask something of Siri using your iPhone, what Siri does consists of five steps: first, speech recognition is used to recognize the words you say. Second, a speech to text process takes place by writing them down. Third, text analysis is done by interpreting the general text. The fourth step is natural language generation by producing a written answer, and finally in the fifth step the text-to-speech responds to your initial question by voice.

Speech recognition is similar to that used in NLP but in addition to understanding natural language and dialects the computer also has to process all the files with different types of voices and sounds using acoustic models.

1.2.2.4 *Natural Language Processing*

Energy companies like those dealing in oil and gas, want to improve operations and keep their employees safe, but this is never easy. Machinery breaks and someone has to fix it. Imagine an employee 200 feet in the air on an icy oil rig. These repairs are not only expensive but also dangerous.

Now companies know that by better analyzing their data, they can improve their operations and thereby save money and keeping their employees safer. However, there is a challenge, as only 20% of the data needed for this analysis are in a structured format like spreadsheets or databases, that is, the data that computers usually use. The other 80% of it is in the form of text such as repair manuals, injury reports and notes jotted down by technicians. This information is extremely valuable but due to its size and structure it has largely been invisible to analytics teams. Imagine if an employee is searching a database of injury reports, and wants to find lower body injuries, the search process will carry out an analysis from one large utility company which showed that lower body injuries returned only a small number of results which was far fewer than actually existed. However, in reality that is because their search tool was looking for the exact keywords "lower body injuries" but when the analysts use more specific search terms such as "foot injuries" they returned many more results where foot was used in the distance between texts. Therefore, while they had more results than searching for just lower body injuries, they weren't the results. This was because a foot can be both a body part and a unit of measurement, and while humans can determine context and understand the difference until recently computers were largely stumped. Thanks to this field of AI called natural language processing (NLP) computers can now analyze and understand textual data [16]. Now let us see how natural language processing works at a high level. NLP algorithms cannot read text like humans do, but they can look for patterns and they find these patterns by turning huge amounts of text into matrices. When analyzing text, the algorithm might first remove words that don't really offer as much value stuff such as "a," "the," "is," "an." These are called stop words. After this, they might split the sentences into groups of words and count how many times each group of words appears in each document and how many documents have that group of words out of all the documents being analyzed without knowing anything at all about the text. The algorithm can then tell how often a given word or phrase appears in a given document and how many documents contain that phrase out of all of the documents. Therefore, tokens that appears lots of times in lots of documents may not mean much, but tokens that appear frequently in only a few documents tell us that something is going on. When combining vast amounts of data and advanced NLP algorithms, a development company called Spark-Cognition found tremendous improvements in operational efficiency and safety [17]. Wind turbine operators are finding the meaning in the data and making that available. Oil and gas operators are able to ask natural language questions when performing diagnostics before repairs. Therefore, with advanced technology like deep NLP from Spark Cognition, a person can now unlock the value of the unstructured data. Every email and every maintenance log in every injury report become real insights that can drive revenue and reduce costs.

1.2.2.5   *Image Analysis*

In the image analysis process, a standard CCTV camera can be used to analyze the images received from CCTV cameras using artificial intelligence and machine learning technologies. The advantages of this technology are that it is reliable, efficient and provides automation capabilities to enable city-wide surveillance solutions. The video analyses done are applicable to vehicles for traffic management and parking, people and objects. In the case of vehicles, traffic management applications, parking applications and picking up incidents within the traffic management apply. For people, the analysis can be done to recognize people so technology can be applied to many different applications. In terms of use cases, such as security smart city in terms of parking and managing big events, retail solutions, industrial zones, transportation, disaster management, in these cases moving pictures allow in detection of different behaviors of people, objects and vehicles. Solutions can be created which can recognize abnormal situations and recognize unsafe and dangerous situations. Face recognition technology is one of the most efficient methods to detect individuals. Recognition technologies can recognize 1 million images in one second in a normal server. Therefore, it provides a fairly high-speed search and is applicable for real-time applications. This technology is able to see through disguises such as headgear and eyeglasses, in crowded situations and also where people are facing different directions. One application of face detection is able to count the number of people in a shopping mall. This can be done using image analysis, and the flow of people can also be tracked. The application can be very useful in detecting the flow of people to and from a bus, providing retail solutions, particularly for the layout of shops in a shopping mall indicating where the best attention grabbers should be sited.

This can be a front-end user interface which can provide off-the-shelf or other third-party solutions. Image search applications can be applied to any platform that the customer may have. For example, in a road traffic management solution, recognition of different kinds of road users can be carried out. The technology can be applied to detect the flow of different road users and also the flow of traffic. In road/ traffic management, 100 cameras can automatically detect different kinds of problems in the road space, including congestion and breakdowns. Dangerous driving, such as reverse driving on a highway, can be automatically detected and alerts sent to the necessary traffic authorities, making this a very important application for road surveillance.

1.2.2.6   *Machine Learning*

Our ability to learn and get better at tasks through experience is part of being human. When we are born, we know almost nothing and can do almost nothing for ourselves, but soon we are learning and becoming more capable every day. Similarly, computers can do the same. Machine learning brings together statistics and computer science to enable computers to learn how to carry out a given task without being programmed to do so [18]. Just as our brains use experience to improve performance in a task, so can computers. A computer can tell the difference between a picture of a dog and a picture of a cat. This can be done by feeding the computer with images and telling it which is a dog, and which is a cat. A computer programmed to learn will seek statistical patterns within the data that will enable it to recognize a cat or dog. In the future it might figure out on its own that cats have shorter noses and dogs come in a larger variety of sizes, and then represent that information numerically an organizing space but, crucially, it is the computer and not the programmer that identifies those patterns and establishes the algorithm by which future data will be sorted. One example of a simple yet highly effective algorithm is to find the optimal line separating cats from dogs. When the computer sees a new picture, it checks which side of the line it falls on and then decides that it is either a cat or a dog. There can, of course, be mistakes. The more data the computer receives, the more finely tuned its algorithm becomes and the more accurate can be its predictions. Machine learning is already widely applied. This is the technology behind facial recognition, text to speech recognition, spam filters in an email inbox, online shopping or viewing recommendations, credit card fraud detection and so much more. Many scientists and machine learning researchers around the globe are combining statistics and computer science to build algorithms that can solve more complex problems, more efficiently, using less computing power. From medical diagnosis to social media the potential of machine learning to transform our world is truly mind-blowing.

1.2.2.7 *Deep Learning*

Deep learning is a subset of machine learning, which in turn is a subset of artificial intelligence. Artificial intelligence is a technique that enables a machine to mimic human behavior. Machine learning is a technique to achieve AI through algorithms trained with data, and finally deep learning is a type of machine learning inspired by the structure of the human brain in terms of deep learning. This structure is called an artificial neural network. Let us understand deep learning better and how it is different from machine learning. For example, say we create a machine that can differentiate between tomatoes and cherries. If carried out using machine learning we would have to tell the machine the features based on which the two can be differentiated. These features could be the size of the fruit and the type of stem. With deep learning, on the other hand, the features are selected by the neural network without human intervention. However, this kind of independence comes at the cost of having a much higher volume of data to train the machine. Now let's look into the working of neural networks as shown in Figure 1.2; here

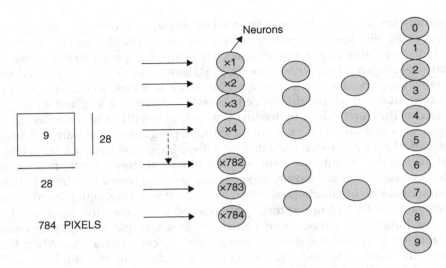

FIGURE 1.2
Working of neural networks.

we have three students each of whom writes down the digit "9" on a piece of paper, notably they don't all write it identically.

The human brain can easily recognize the digits, but what if a computer had to recognize them? That's where deep learning comes in. In the figure there is a neural network trained to identify handwritten digits, and each number is present as an image of 28 ×28 pixels, which amounts to a total of 784 pixel neurons. The core entity of a neural network is where the information processing takes place. Each of the 784 pixels is fed into a neuron in the first layer of the neural network, which will form the input layer [19]. Meanwhile, on the other end we have the output layer with each neuron representing a digit with the hidden layers existing between them. The information transforms one layer to another over connecting channels. Each of these channels has a value attached to it, and hence is called a weighted channel. Each neuron has a unique number associated with it, called the bias. This bias is added to the weighted sum of inputs reaching the neuron, which is then applied to a function known as the activation function. The result of the activation function determines whether the neuron gets activated. Every activated neuron passes on information to the following layers. This process continues up till the second last layer. The one neuron activated in the output layer corresponds to the input digit. The weights and bias are continuously adjusted to produce a well-trained network. Now let's see where deep learning can be applied. In customer support, when most people converse with customer support agents the conversation seems so real that they don't even realize that it's actually a bot on the other side. Also, in medical care, neural networks detect cancer cells and analyze MRI images to give detailed results. In self-driving cars, what seems like science fiction is now a reality with companies like Apple, Tesla and Nissan being only a few of the companies working on self-driving cars. Therefore deep learning has vast scope although it also faces some limitations. The first, as we discussed earlier, is data, while deep learning is the most efficient way to deal with unstructured data. A neural network requires a massive volume of data to train. Let's assume we always have access to the necessary amount of data processing. This is not within the capability of every machine, which brings us to the second limitation. The computational power training and neural network requires graphical processing units which have thousands of courses as compared to CPUs and GPUs, which are of course more expensive, and finally we come down to the training time, with deep neural networks taking hours or even months to train. The time increases with the amount of data and number of layers in the network. Some of the popular deep learning frameworks include TensorFlow, Pytorch and Keras.

1.2.2.8 Cognition

International Data Corporation (IDC) has defined cognitive artificial intelligence [20]. AI systems are a set of technologies that use deep natural language processing and understanding to answer questions and provide recommendations and direction. Artificial intelligence (AI) is one of the components of a cognitive application that contributes to machine learning from data and making decisions, suggestions or discoveries. Cognitive AI consists of machines that strive for human capacity using digital intelligence learning from human-created dark data and reasoning to make decisions with the mindset to emulate the human thought process and produce similar results [21]. There are two different fields of cognitive AI: supervised and unsupervised. Supervised AI starts from a generic industry-specific model or framework. For each customer the model is manually updated and customized by a team of human data scientists. This method is time and resource intensive, and is not scalable. Unsupervised AI creates models that are uniquely client specific, meaning no two models are exactly alike. Human interference is not needed for the learning phase. The key characteristics of unsupervised methods are that the technology is language agnostic, and the technology learns in the language that the data come in, just like a human native speaker. The technology learns and reasons based on observing or ingesting the best human-created data continuously learning more. This method is scalable as the needs of the organization increase. The model automatically updates to include new information without human intervention.

Some cases are described to illustrate several examples of how organizations around the world are utilizing unsupervised cognitive computing. We can look at customer support, for example, routing in the traditional or non-cognitive way. The process begins when a customer submits a service ticket which arrives at an agent who must then select the best suited competency center. An agent process ensures that the customer ticketing and repays if it is incorrectly processed. The agent then routes the ticket to a competency center. The receiving agent processes the requests, sometimes taking up to seven days to issue a decision. Finally, the agent's answer is received by the customer. Companies use cognitive RPA to augment the traditional routing method. The solution is micro-routing, the benefit of this solution is that when the service ticket is received the queue robot routes it directly to the best suited department specialist, accelerating the speed of service and giving the specialist the agency to provide their best service to their customers over time as the loop queue continuously observes and learns from human employees and is able to predict the likely answer to inbound requests based on the outcomes of passed similar tickets and by utilizing the confidence level. This is a great solution for accommodating the learning curves of new employees and standardizing the service of all agents depending on the client's wishes answers can come in one of two forms. Fully automated answers sent directly to customers are based on the confidence level with a threshold set by the client, or a list of answer options is created for human agents to select from. Moving on to another popular use case, there is some knowledge that one can only gain by hands-on experience which is not written in any manual or procedure. When employees leave a company that precious knowledge goes with them. The employees' corporate knowledge is locked away in emails, old notes, manuals, training documents, reports, decision logs and documents. It is in a variety of styles, formats and often many languages. Loop Q is able to obtain all of that information and build a cortex to be used for applications such as cognitive search with the tribal knowledge solution.

Currently, digital technologies are doing for human brain power what steam engines and related technologies did for human muscle power during the Industrial Revolution. They are allowing us to overcome many limitations rapidly and to open up new frontiers with unprecedented speed. There are many operational benefits to be had with the support of AI, including increased productivity, giving human agents the speed and accuracy to handle cases better. Human agents can now handle a higher volume of cases per day, easily scaling to meet the demands of their customers. Now, human agents are sharp and compliant in their decision-making and company regulations and administrative processes are better at assessing risk.. With more information and better fraud detection, human agents can be better prepared to assess risk. Employee benefits are also increased with the support of AI. Better engagement is obtained with digital employees gathering information and presenting it to human employees. Human agents are able to deeply interact with each case, giving their full attention to the details for the best possible customer service with the information readily available. Human agents thus feel less stress and pressure to search for and discover the correct answer.

1.3 An Evolution of Blockchain Mechanism through Distributed Transaction

As an emerging distributed computing paradigm and decentralized architecture, blockchain has gained intensive attention in various sectors. Also, the significant benefit of blockchain technology lies in enabling the trusted, secured and decentralized autonomous ecosystems for different scenarios, exclusively for the better utilization of infrastructure, devices and resources. Moreover, it is a primitive technology for the evolving cryptocurrencies and the main benefit of blockchain technology is widely contemplated to be decentralized. It assists in establishing peer-to-peer (P2P) transactions and coordination among distributed systems without any centralized coordinator between individual nodes based on distributed consensus algorithms, incentive mechanisms, data encryption and time-stamping. Furthermore, blockchain can provide an incredible solution for long-term problems such as low efficiency, high operational costs and potential risks in maintaining data following a centralized approach. Blockchain is identified as a disruptive innovative technology in the computer paradigm after personal computer (PC), mainframe, mobile networks and social networks. It is anticipated that blockchain will radically reform the behavioral model of several organizations and individuals, consequently realizing the transition toward its future usage [22].

The rapidly increasing trend of blockchain has gained huge attention from different sectors such as financial institutions, governments, capital markets and high-tech enterprises. Blockchain is defined as a shared distributed ledger that practices encrypted, chronological and chained blocks to maintain synchronized and verifiable data (e.g., states, behavior, transactions, decisions, etc.) across the network. It is also viewed as a distributed and decentralized computing paradigm, which stores data in the form of encrypted chained blocks, data are verified with consensus algorithms, guaranteeing the data transmission process with cryptographic techniques, and manipulating data with smart contracts.

Blockchain has several desirable characteristics in organizational and technical aspects such as reliable, trustable, efficient, usable, autonomous, automated, decentralized and distributed. In particular, blockchain is witnessed as a distributed shared ledger, where the blockchain data can be recorded, verified, stored, maintained and transmitted. In this distributed platform, mutual trust is established among the distributed nodes using mathematical algorithms without any intervention of third- party authorities. The transactional data are maintained in the structure of chained blocks along with time stamps, which enables robust verifiability and traceability of blockchain data with its temporal dimension. The different incentive mechanisms are introduced to crowdsource the blockchain mining process in order to increase the figure of blockchain miners. Moreover, the miners can contribute and verify the data blocks which are maintained in the distributed shared ledger and compete to win the opportunity to create the next data block and add it to the main blockchain in the consensus process. Blockchain is also influenced by programmable codes and scripts, hence users can generate cryptocurrencies, smart contracts, or decentralized applications (DApps). For example, the Ethereum platform provides scripting language that helps users to design any transaction or smart contract. Finally, the blockchain data are encrypted and secured using asymmetric cryptography among a huge number of distributed nodes in the blockchain network. The blockchain is considered to be a secured platform, thus it protects the complete process from outside attackers and also ensures robust non-tamperability and non-forgeability. Blockchain is a primitive technical framework which brings a string of influence to the economics, finance, politics, and science and technological domains.

The key characteristics that make the blockchain network more trusted are:

- Ledger: The blockchain technology enables participants to append a ledger rather than overriding values and transactions in a blockchain, thus providing the complete transaction history.
- Distributed: The blockchain network facilitates scalability to increase the number of nodes, which automatically reduces the impact of attackers on the consensus mechanism.
- Shared: The ledger is distributed and shared among participants involved in the blockchain network, thus alleviating transparency.
- Secure: The data maintained in the ledger cannot be tampered with and can be verified because blockchain networks are cryptographically well secured.

Some of the terminologies related to blockchain technology are:

- Blockchain: this term refers to the actual ledger.
- Blockchain user: entity, organization, government, business, a person, etc.
- Node: this refers to the individual system in the blockchain network. There are two categories of nodes, namely, full node and lightweight node.

    i.   Full node: This is a node that maintains the complete blockchain, guaranteeing that all transactions are valid. The publishing node is a kind of full node that can publish new blocks.

    ii.   Lightweight node: This is a node which does not maintain the copy of transactions and simply passes the transactions to the full node.

1.3.1 General Categories of Blockchain

Blockchain is generally categorized as permissioned and permissionless based on the permission model. In a permissioned blockchain, participation is limited based on some constraints and can be deployed by specific organizations or individuals. This means that only a particular set of users can publish their blocks. Permissionless blockchain allows anyone to publish (read/write) a new block without any authorization. For example, a permissioned blockchain is similar to a controlled corporate intranet, whereas a permissionless blockchain is similar to the public Internet which permits anyone to participate.

1.3.1.1 Permissioned Blockchain

The publishing blocks in the permissioned blockchain must be authorized by someone (centralized/decentralized authorities). Only authorized users maintain the blockchain, read access and issuing transactions could be restricted in this permissioned blockchain. It may permit/restrict read access to any authorized individuals or group of individuals. It may allow/restrict individuals to submit transactions. This kind of network can be implemented using open or closed source software. The digital assets are traced when passed via the blockchain, these are resilient, redundant and distributed data storage systems. Consensus models are exploited to publish new blocks, although they do not require any expense or resource maintenance. Consensus models incur less computational cost and are commonly faster in permissioned blockchains. The organizations that necessitate rigid protection and control can preferably incorporate permissioned blockchain. The authorized participants can publish new blocks and the authorization could be revoked if the organization uncovers any misbehavior. The permission blockchain can be established to invite various business partners and the transactions can be recorded on a shared ledger. Beyond trust, it also facilitates transparency and deep insight to make better business decisions periodically, and misbehaving entities can be tracked easily in the permissioned blockchain network.

  In the permissioned blockchain, transactional information can be revealed selectively based on user credentials or identity; hence a certain degree of privacy can be obtained. All participants in the permissioned blockchain need to be authorized for sending and receiving transactions. If any misbehaving activities occur, it is easy to track and employ the legal remedies according to the suitable judicial system.

1.3.1.2 Permissionless Blockchain

Permissionless blockchains are decentralized open-source platforms, where anyone can publish their blocks without obtaining permission from authorities. There is no restriction in reading/writing and issuing transactions in this type of blockchain. To prevent malicious activities, a consensus mechanism is utilized in the permissionless blockchain which requires maintenance or expenditure of resources while making an attempt to publish new blocks.

1.3.2 Key Components of Blockchain Technology

Blockchain technology seems to be complex, yet it could be simplified by understanding the components individually. Blockchain technology implements several cryptographic mechanisms, such as asymmetric cryptography, hash function and digital signature. The significant components in blockchain technology are:

- asymmetric key cryptography
- hash function
- address
- transaction
- ledger
- block.

1.3.2.1 Asymmetric Key Cryptography

Blockchain technology exploits public-key cryptography, known as asymmetric-key cryptography, which exercises both a private and a public key. Also, the public key is declared as public without compromising the security level; however, the private key is required to be kept secret always. It is difficult to determine the private key by knowing the public key, encrypt using the private key or decrypt using the public key; instead encrypting uses the public key and decrypting uses the private key. The asymmetric cryptography builds a trust relationship among users by verifying the authenticity and integrity of transactions by remaining public. In particular, the transactions are maintained as a "digitally signed" copy; encrypting transactions requires a private key such that it can be decrypted by anyone exploiting the public key. Otherwise, data are encrypted using a public key and it could be decrypted using their private key. The main disadvantage of asymmetric cryptography is that the computational process may be too slow. A single key known as a "secret key" or "shared key" is used in symmetric cryptography. A secret key is shared via trusted media with each other. In symmetric cryptography, data are encrypted using a shared key and decrypted only using the shared key. The advantage of symmetric cryptography is fast computational processes. The utilization of asymmetric cryptography in a blockchain network is as follows:

- Private keys: digital signing of transactions.
- Public keys: verifying signatures that are created using private keys.
- Public keys: to obtain addresses also.

Several permissioned blockchain leverage public-key infrastructures are required to afford user credentials rather than managing the user's own asymmetric keys. A blockchain network utilizes directory services by implementing the Lightweight Directory Access Protocol (LDAP) to use the existing information from the directory.

1.3.2.2 Hash Function

Hashing is a technique that produces a "digest" or "message digest" for any size input (e.g., text, file or image). The changes in an input result in a different message digest after hashing the given data. Some of the significant properties of hash functions are pre-image resistant and collision resistant. In pre-image resistant, one-way communication is enabled, which means that it is computationally difficult to compute the input from the output digest [e.g., finding "a" from hash (a) = digest]. Second pre-image resistant means that it is computationally difficult to interpret the second input which resulted in the same output [e.g., given a, finding b where hash (a) = hash (b)]. In collision resistant, it is computationally difficult to find two inputs which resulted in the same output [e.g., finding a and b where hash (a) = hash (b)]. A nonce is an arbitrary pseudo random number along with input data given for the hash function to create the digest as an output. The different nonce values for the same input produce various message digest values. The cryptographic nonce technique is followed in the Proof-of-Work (PoW) consensus mechanism. A hash function called the Secure Hash Algorithm (SHA) with 256 bits output (SHA-256) is incorporated in various blockchain implementations. SHA-256 produces 32 bytes of output (256 bits) in 64-character digits hexadecimal format (as shown in Table 1.1).

The hash function accomplishes the following tasks in the blockchain network:

- Secures the block header and data
- Creates unique identifiers
- Derives an address.

TABLE 1.1

Sample Input Text and Its Digest Values Using SHA-256

Input Text	Digest Values (SHA-256)
10	0x4a44dc15364204a80fe80e9039455cc1608281820fe2b24f1e5233ade6af1dd5
20	0xf5ca38f748a1d6eaf726b8a42fb575c3c71f1864a8143301782de13da2d9202b
Welcome!!!	0xd2c8af45b8232023f7bf74ce15398d16c2caef70934449fe3406dcc1d286a1b0

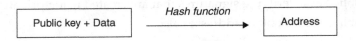

FIGURE 1.3
Finding an address in blockchain.

1.3.2.3 Address

The address in the blockchain network is an alphanumeric character string obtained from the public key of the user along with some input data using a hash function, as depicted in Figure 1.3.

The addresses in the blockchain network can be derived using different methodologies. For example, a permissionless blockchain system permits users to generate asymmetric key pairs for as many addresses as desired. It acts as an identifier for a user in the blockchain network. In the Ethereum platform, smart contracts are available using special addresses by creating a contract account. The account address is computed and generated, and permits the contract to be executed once the transaction is received. The wallet is software that acts as a private key storage to secure and manage the user's private keys in the blockchain network. It can store private and public keys along with their associated addresses. In addition, it computes the whole sum of digital assets that each user possesses.

1.3.2.4 Transaction

A transaction refers to the interaction among participants, i.e., transferring cryptocurrency between network participants. Figure 1.4 shows the transaction of cryptocurrencies, where each block may have zero/more transactions in a blockchain. The sender in a blockchain sends the information by including the sender's public key, sender's address, a digital signature, and the input and output of a transaction [23]. The minimum requirements for each cryptocurrency transaction are:

i.   Input: The list of digital assets is considered as an input for the transaction. The input of the current transaction is completely dependent

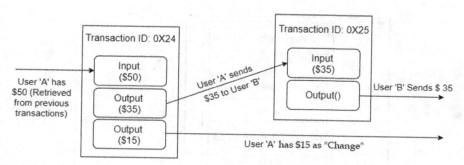

FIGURE 1.4

Transaction of cryptocurrencies.

on the past event. Also, the values cannot be updated in the existing asset, instead they can be split or merged to form a new asset.

ii. Output: This is the recipient of the amount which is received, and it refers to the number of assets which are transferred to the next owner.

1.3.2.5 Ledger

A ledger is a list of all the transactions that have occurred. By design, a blockchain network produces several backup copies of the same ledger records, which are all modified and synchronized among peers. One of the main advantages of blockchain technology is that each user can keep their own copy of the distributed ledger. When new nodes enter the blockchain network, they search out other full nodes and demand the complete copy of the blockchain network's distributed ledger, which makes it impossible to lose or break the ledger.

1.3.2.6 Block

Whenever a publishing node releases a block, transactions are recorded on the blockchain. A block is made up of two parts: (i) a block header and (ii) block data. This metadata information of each block is stored in the block header and is shown in Figure 1.5. A list of validated transactions has been published to the blockchain network and is included in the block data. Validity is assured by verifying that the transaction is properly formatted and that each of the digital asset providers has cryptographically signed the transaction.

In the block header, the following details are maintained:

- Block number (also called block height)
- Hash value of previous block header

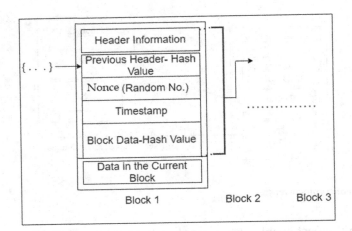

FIGURE 1.5
Chain of blocks.

- Block data
- Timestamp
- Block size
- Nonce value.

Also, the list of transactions (ledger events) in the region of the block data.

References

1. Raj, P., T. Poongodi, B. Balusamy, and M. Khari (Eds.) (2020). *The Internet of Things and Big Data Analytics: Integrated Platforms and Industry Use Cases*. CRC Press, Boca Raton, FL.
2. Sethi, P., and S. R. Sarangi (2017). Internet of things: Architectures, protocols, and applications. *Journal of Electrical and Computer Engineering 2017*, 1–26.
3. Poongodi, T., A. Rathee, R. Indrakumari, and P. Suresh (2020). IoT sensing capabilities: Sensor deployment and node discovery, wearable sensors, wireless body area network (WBAN), data acquisition. In Sheng-Lung Peng, Souvik Pal, Lianfen Huang (eds) *Principles of Internet of Things (IoT) Ecosystem: Insight Paradigm*, pp. 127–151. Springer, Cham, Switzerland.
4. Poongodi, T., T. Agnesbeena, S. Janarthanan, and B. Balamurugan (2020). Accelerating data acquisition process in the pharmaceutical industry using Internet of Things. *An Industrial IoT Approach for Pharmaceutical Industry Growth*, 2, 117.

5. Muro, M., R. Maxim, and J. Whiton (2019). *Automation and Artificial Intelligence: How Machines Are Affecting People and Places*. http://hdl.handle.net/11540/9686

6. Acemoglu, D., and P. Restrepo (2018). Artificial intelligence, automation, and work. In *The economics of artificial intelligence: An agenda* (pp. 197–236). University of Chicago Press, Chicago.

7. Chilamkurti, N., T. Poongodi, and B. Balusamy (Eds.) (2021). *Blockchain, Internet of Things, and Artificial Intelligence*. CRC Press, Boca Raton, FL.

8. Apolloni, B., W. Pedrycz, S. Bassis, and D. Malchiodi (2008). Knowledge engineering. In *The Puzzle of Granular Computing*, pp. 411–449. Springer, Berlin, Heidelberg.

9. Henrion, M., J. S. Breese, and E. J. Horvitz (1991). Decision analysis and expert systems. *AI Magazine*, 12(4), 64.

10. Macías-Escrivá, F. D., R. Haber, R. Del Toro, and V. Hernandez (2013). Self-adaptive systems: A survey of current approaches, research challenges and applications. *Expert Systems with Applications*, 40(18), 7267–7279.

11. Richards, D. (2009). A social software/Web 2.0 approach to collaborative knowledge engineering. *Information Sciences*, 179(15), 2515–2523.

12. Madakam, S., R. M. Holmukhe, and D. K. Jaiswal (2019). The future digital work force: Robotic process automation (RPA). *JISTEM-Journal of Information Systems and Technology Management*, 16, 1–16.

13. Aguirre, S., and A. Rodriguez (September 2017). Automation of a business process using robotic process automation (RPA): A case study. In Juan Carlos Figueroa-Garcia, Eduyn Ramiro Lopez- Santana, Jose Luis Villa-Ramirez, Roberto Ferro-Escobar (eds) *Workshop on Engineering Applications*, pp. 65–71. Springer, Cham, Switzerland.

14. Conn, S. (2017). Gartner says by 2020, artificial intelligence will create more jobs than it eliminates, *Gartner*. Available at: www.gartner.com/en/newsroom/press-releases/2017-12-13-gartner-says-by-2020-artificial-intelligence-will-create-more-jobs-than-it-eliminates

15. Halle, M., and K. Stevens (1962). Speech recognition: A model and a program for research. *IRE Transactions on Information Theory*, 8(2), 155–159.

16. Liu, D., Y. Li, and M. A. Thomas (2017). A roadmap for natural language processing research in information systems. In *Proceedings of the 50th Hawaii International Conference on System Sciences (2017)*. Hawaii International Conference on System Sciences.

17. Herve Philippe, R. M. (2017). Oil & gas and natural language processing are the perfect match no one predicted | sparkcognition, inc., *Spark Cognition*. Available at: www.sparkcognition.com/oil-gas-natural-language-processing-are-perfect-match-no-one-predicted/

18. Jordan, M. I., and T. M. Mitchell (2015). Machine learning: Trends, perspectives, and prospects, *Science*, 349. American Association for the Advancement of Science, 255–260. doi: 10.1126/science.aaa8415

19. Mikkel, Duif (2019). Exploring how neural networks work and visualising them, *Towards Data Science*. Available at: https://towardsdatascience.com/exploring-how-neural-networks-work-and-making-them-interactive-ed67adbf9283

20. Adadi, A., and M. Berrada (2018). Peeking inside the black-box: A survey on explainable artificial intelligence (xai). *IEEE Access*, 6, 52138–52160.

21. Claudé, M., and D. Combe (2018). *The Roles of Artificial Intelligence and Humans in Decision Making: Towards Augmented Humans?: A Focus on Knowledge-Intensive Firms.* Umea University.

22. Poongodi, T., R. Sujatha, D. Sumathi, P. Suresh, and B. Balamurugan (2020). Blockchain in social networking. *Cryptocurrencies and Blockchain Technology Applications* (pp. 55–76). Wiley, Hoboken, NJ.

23. Poongodi, T., R. Indrakumari, M. Kiruthika, S. Suganthi, and P. Suresh (2021). Blockchain technology and its relevance in healthcare. In Poongodi, T., R. Indrakumari, M. Kiruthika, S. Suganthi, and P. Suresh (eds) *Blockchain and Machine Learning for E-Healthcare Systems*, IET, 1–25. IET Digital Library.

2

Basic Fundamentals of the Internet of Things, Artificial Intelligence and Blockchain

The entities in the Internet of Things (IoT) require diverse sets of standards and protocols to enable communication over a network. The communication technologies include RFID (radio frequency identification), NFC (near-field communication), Bluetooth, Zigbee, Wi-Fi, etc. and are meant for short-, medium- and long-range communication. The architectural framework integrates components for their seamless cooperation among each other to solve complex tasks. AI systems are capable of learning which facilitates improvements of their performance over time. AI tools include machine learning, predictive analysis and deep learning, which increase the ability for learning, reasoning, thinking and decision-making. Furthermore, the future predictions for AI are explored in depth and potential solutions are recommended to solve the problems faced in the coming decades. Blockchain is an open-source hyperledger to track the provenance of different items in many sectors such as healthcare, manufacturing, retail industry, finance and insurance, etc. The convergence of these technologies has become vital, beneficial and inevitable in the fourth digital revolution.

2.1 Basic Framework and Architecture of the Internet of Things

The IoT facilitates physical objects to listen, hear, think and perform tasks by allowing them to interact with one another, exchange information and make decisions. By using primary technologies such as ubiquitous and widespread computing, embedded devices, networking technologies, wireless sensor networks (WSNs), IPs and other applications, generally the IoT transforms these smart things from conventional to smart. Domain-specific applications (vertical markets) are made up of smart objects and their supposed functionalities, whereas domain-independent applications are made up of ubiquitous computing and analytical services (horizontal markets). In that case, if a domain-specific IoT application communicates with domain-independent

DOI: 10.1201/9781003046462-3

services, sensors and actuators in each domain interact directly with one another. Further, the IoT is anticipated to have substantial commercial applications in the future, leading to enhanced quality of life and global economic development. Smart homes, for example, would allow residents to unlock their garage doors automatically when they arrive home, make coffee, and control TVs, automated climate control and other appliances.

Emerging technologies and developments, as well as service implementations, must expand proportionately to market demands and consumer needs in order to realize the capacity for rapid growth. Furthermore, devices must be designed to meet consumer needs for accessibility anywhere and at any time. To obtain compatibility among heterogeneous objects during communication, new protocols are also required (living beings, goods, phones, automated vehicles, appliances, etc.). Furthermore, standard architecture can be seen as a spine for the IoT, allowing businesses to compete by delivering high-quality goods.

Moreover, conventional Internet architecture must be updated to meet the IoT challenges. Many underlying protocols, for example, should take into account where an immense number of objects are ready to link to the Internet. In 2010, the number of Internet-linked smart objects overtook the global human population. As a result, to satisfy consumer demands for smart objects, a wide addressing space (e.g., IPv6) is required. Because of the inherent heterogeneity of smart objects and the capability to track and manipulate physical entities, security and privacy are the most important criteria for IoT systems. Furthermore, IoT systems should be managed and controlled so as to guarantees that high-quality services are provided to consumers at less cost.

2.1.1 Basic Components of the IoT System

Recognizing the IoT basic building components will assist in achieving a better understanding of the IoT's nature and functionality. The six key elements required to deliver IoT functionality are discussed in the following sections, as outlined in Table 2.1.

TABLE 2.1

Components of the IoT and Its Relevant Technologies

IoT Elements	Technologies
Identification	uCode, EPC—Naming
	IPv4, IPv6—Addressing
Sensing	RFID tag, sensors, actuators, smart sensors, embedded sensors, etc.
Communication	Bluetooth, Wi-Fi, BLE, RFID, NFC, UWB, Z-Wave
Computation	Arduino, Beagle Bone, Z1, UDOO, Intel Galileo, Raspberry PI, etc.
Services	Identity, information aggregation, collaborative aware, ubiquitous
Semantics	Knowledge extraction tools (OWL, RDF, etc.)

2.1.1.1 *Identification*

Identification is critical in IoT systems for naming and matching services on demand. There are a number of IoT identification methods available, including electronic product codes (EPCs) and ubiquitous codes (uCode). In addition, addressing smart objects in IoT systems is crucial by distinguishing the object identifier and address. The object identifier is the name of an object including T1 for a specific temperature sensor, and the address is its position within a communications network. IPv6 and IPv4 are also used as addressing methods for IoT objects. 6LoWPAN uses an IPv6 header compression method that makes it ideal for low-power consumption wireless networks. Since identifying methods are not globally specific, distinguishing among object identifiers and addresses is critical. Addressing helps in identifying objects in a unique manner. Furthermore, objects on the network can use public IP addresses rather than private addresses. Identification mechanisms are exploited to give each object in the network a distinct identity.

2.1.1.2 *Sensing*

Sensing in an IoT environment means gathering data from the connected objects and transmitting them to a data warehouse, database or the cloud. Also, the information gathered is evaluated in order to proceed with appropriate actions based on the services required. Smart sensors, actuators and wearable sensing systems are examples of IoT sensors. Several companies, for example, provide smart applications that permit people to use their smartphones to track and manage thousands of smart appliances within buildings. To build IoT devices, single-board computers (SBCs) with sensors, security functions and in-built TCP/IP are commonly used (e.g., Raspberry PI, Arduino, etc.). Customers usually request data from such devices, which are connected to a central management server.

2.1.1.3 *Communication*

The communication technologies allow heterogeneous objects to communicate with one another in order to provide precise smart services. With the existence of noisy communication links, IoT nodes can typically operate at low power. IEEE 802.15.4, Wi-Fi, Bluetooth, LTE-Advanced and Z-wave, are examples of IoT networking protocols. RFID, ultra-wide bandwidth (UWB) and near-field communication (NFC) are communication technologies that are also used. RFID (tag and reader) was the primary technology to bring the M2M idea into practice. The RFID tag is a simple chip that is fixed to an item to identify it. Also, the RFID reader sends a signal to the tag and then obtains a reflected signal, which is then sent to the database. The database binds to a processing center to classify objects in the range of 10 cm to 200 m based on reflected signals. Active tags, passive tags, and semi-passive and active

RFID tags are available. Batteries are required for active tags, but they are not required for passive tags. The NFC protocol operates at 13.56 MHz in the high-frequency band and supports a 424 kbps data rate. The communication among active readers and passive tags/two active readers is possible within a range of up to 10 cm. The UWB technology has been developed to facilitate communications within a short-range coverage area while using high bandwidth and low energy, and its applications to link such kinds of sensors have grown substantially.

Wi-Fi is another networking technology in which radio waves are used to send and receive data within a 100-meter range. In certain ad hoc configurations, Wi-Fi permits smart devices to connect and share information even without the use of a router. Bluetooth is a communication technology that uses short-wavelength radio to transfer data among devices within short distances with minimum power consumption. Bluetooth 4.1 was recently announced by the Bluetooth Special Interest Group (SIG), and includes Bluetooth Low Energy with high-speed network connectivity that is a provision of IoT systems. Also, the IEEE 802.15.4 specification describes a physical layer as well as a medium access control protocol for low-power wireless networks that increases the scalability and reliability of communication. Next, LTE (Long-Term Evolution) is another wireless communication protocol function focusing on GSM/UMTS network technologies for data transmission at a high speed among mobile phones. It has the ability to cover fast-moving devices while also providing broadcasting and multicasting facilities. LTE-A (LTE Advanced) is a more advanced variant of LTE that includes up to 100 MHz of bandwidth expansion, spatial multiplexing, lower latency, better throughput and extended coverage.

2.1.1.4 Computation

The significant computational abilities of the IoT system are represented as processing units (e.g., microprocessors, microcontrollers, etc.) and other software applications. Arduino, BeagleBone, Z1, UDOO, Intel Galileo, Mulle, Raspberry PI, FriendlyARM, Gadgeteer, T-Mote Sky, Cubieboard and WiSense are some of the hardware platforms that have been established to execute IoT applications. Moreover, a variety of software interfaces are used to provide IoT functionality. Operating systems (RTOS) are critical among these platforms because they function for the duration of a device's activation. Several real-time operating systems (RTOS) are suitable for the production of IoT applications based on RTOS.

The Contiki RTOS, for example, is commonly exploited in IoT-based circumstances. Also, Contiki has a Cooja simulator that enables researchers and developers to simulate IoT and wireless sensor network (WSN) applications. LiteOS, TinyOS and Riot OS are all lightweight operating systems developed for the IoT. Furthermore, the Open Auto Alliance (OAA) was established by auto industry leaders and Google, with the aim of introducing additional characteristics to the Android platform to speed up the adoption of the Internet of Vehicles (IoV) paradigm.

2.1.1.5 Services

Generally, IoT services can be characterized into four categories: (a) identity-related services; (b) information aggregation services; (c) collaborative-aware services and (d) ubiquitous services.

a)   Identity-based services are the significant primary services that are exploited in various kinds of services. Any application that desires to carry real-world objects into the virtual world must find them initially.

b)   Information-aggregation services gather and review the sensory measurements which are required in IoT applications.

c)   Collaborative-aware services are commonly functioned on the top-level of information-aggregation services; the obtained data are used for efficient decision-making and act accordingly.

d)   Ubiquitous services, on the other hand, focus on delivering collaborative-aware services to everyone, anywhere, at any time. Several IoT applications strive to achieve the status of ubiquitous services as their ultimate target.

The information-aggregation category includes smart healthcare and smart grids, while the collaborative-aware type includes smart buildings, smart homes, industrial automation and intelligent transportation networks (ITNs).

Smart home IoT services improve people's lives by making it simpler and more convenient to remotely track and control home appliances and devices (such as heating systems, energy consumption meters, air conditioners, etc.). For example, with weather forecasting applications, a smart home can automatically close the windows and lower the shutters of upstairs windows. Smart homes must interact with both the internal and external surroundings on a regular basis. The internal atmosphere might even include devices and appliances which are connected to the Internet, whereas the external atmosphere might have objects that will not be under the smart home control, such as smart grid entities.

Building automation systems (BASs) are connected to the Internet in smart buildings. A BAS enables the control and management of various devices including HVAC, safety, security, lighting and shading, and entertainment, with the help of sensors and actuators. Moreover, BAS may result in the reduction of energy consumption and building maintenance costs. For instance, a cooling/heating system or a blinking dishwasher may provide an alarm if there is an issue that needs to be investigated and resolved. As a result, requests for maintenance may be submitted to a contracting organization without any human interference.

Intelligent transportation systems (ITSs) track and manage the transportation network by integrating the computation and communication functionalities. The aim of an ITS is to improve the transportation infrastructure's reliability, performance, availability and security. The four significant components in an ITS are:

    i. Monitoring center
   ii. Security subsystem
  iii. Vehicle subsystem (RFID reader, GPS, OBU)
  iv. Station subsystem (road-side devices).

Furthermore, connected vehicles are gaining in popularity as a means of making driving more effective, reliable and enjoyable.

Industrial automation refers to the computerization of robotic systems in order to accomplish production activities with negligible human intervention. Primarily focused on four elements (transportation, sensing, processing and communication), it enables a set of machines to manufacture goods more efficiently and accurately. The role of the IoT in industrial automation is to manage and track the processes, functionalities and output rate of production machines. For example, if a machine encounters a problem suddenly, an IoT device automatically transmits a repair query to the relevant department, which will resolve the problem. In addition, the IoT improves productivity by effectively examining production-related timing, data and root causes of production problems.

Sensors and actuators can be embedded in patients and their medicines can be tracked continuously in smart healthcare applications. Clinical care uses the IoT to track patients' physiological conditions through sensors, which gather and analyze their data, and then send the collected information to processing centers to take appropriate actions. IBM recently used RFID at one of its hospitals to monitor the handwashing system once after completion of the testing process. This activity is performed to prevent diseases, which kill about 90,000 people per year and costs the economy $30 billion.

Smart grids exploit the IoT to increase the energy efficiency of homes and buildings. Furthermore, the IoT in smart grids enables better monitoring and managing of resources by power suppliers. Smart grids, for instance, use the IoT to link a number of building meters to the energy provider's network. And also, energy consumption is recorded, measured, controlled, monitored and handled using these meters. The IoT allows energy suppliers to widen their services in order to meet the needs of their customers. Using the IoT in the smart grid often decreases the risk of failure, improves reliability, and advances service quality also.

A smart city is one of the applications of ubiquitous services, which focuses on promoting life quality in urban areas, that is simpler and highly convenient for people to search relevant information. Various systems are integrated to provide necessary services in smart city surroundings (transportation, utilities, health, government, buildings and homes).

2.1.1.6 Semantics

In the IoT, semantic means the capability of various devices to acquire knowledge intelligently in order to provide the necessary services. Discovering and utilizing tools, as well as modeling data, are all part of knowledge extraction. It also entails identifying and evaluating data in order to provide the correct decision with the best service.

2.1.2 IoT—Layered Architecture

The IoT can normally interconnect billions of heterogeneous devices, hence a versatile layered architecture is essential. The ever-increasing number of proposed architectures has made it difficult to choose a standard one. The primary model is a three-layered architecture composed of the application, network and perception layers, which was chosen from a collection of proposed models. Some other reference models that bring greater refinement to the existing IoT architecture have been proposed recently. Three-layered and five-layered reference models are depicted in Figure 2.1. A discussion on the five-layered model follows.

2.1.2.1 Perception/Object Layer

The perception/object layer is the first layer that characterizes the IoT's sensors to capture and process data. In addition, this layer contains sensors and actuators that can query position, acceleration, motion, weight,

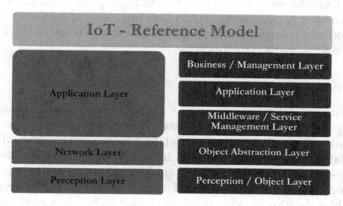

FIGURE 2.1
IoT layered architecture.

temperature, vibration, humidity, etc. [1]. The perception layer uses the standardized plug-and-play mechanisms to configure the objects which are heterogeneous. Also, the perception layer transmits data to the next layer, called the object abstraction layer. Moreover, the generation of big data by IoT devices is also initiated in this layer.

2.1.2.2   Object Abstraction Layer

Object abstraction uses safe channels to transfer data from the previous layer to the next later, the service management layer. RFID, Bluetooth Low Energy (BLE), Wi-Fi, UMTS, GSM, 3G, ZigBee, infrared and other communication technologies can be used to transmit data. Furthermore, other functionalities, such as cloud storage, data management, etc. are also managed at this object abstraction layer.

2.1.2.3   Middleware/Service Management Layer

The middleware/service management layer matches a service with the details of the requester using names and addresses. Also, the middleware layer allows programmers to proceed with their tasks with a variety of heterogeneous entities without exploiting any particular hardware platform. Furthermore, this middleware layer also receives data, processes them by making an efficient decision, and delivers the desired services with the support of network communication protocols.

2.1.2.4   Application Layer

Customers request services, which are generally offered by the application layer. For example, this layer will also provide air humidity and temperature measurements to a customer who requests them. This layer is essential for the IoT system since only it can deliver high-quality services in order to satisfy customer requirements. Smart building, smart healthcare, industrial automation and transportation, smart home, etc. are some of the significant vertical markets covered by this layer.

2.1.2.5   Business/Management Layer

The operations and different services of the complete IoT system are controlled by the management layer. Also, this business layer's responsibilities include creating a business model, graphs, flowcharts and other visual representations of the data obtained from the previous layer. Moreover, it is also responsible for the design, analysis, implementation, evaluation, monitoring and development of IoT device components. In general, this layer enables decision-making processes based on big data analysis and also performs control and management of the remaining four layers under it.

Furthermore, this management layer compares the output of each layer to the planned output for improving services and safeguarding users' privacy.

Finally, it is concluded that the application layer acts as an interface from which the users can communicate with a computer and demand the desired data in the five-layer model. It also connects to the business/management layer, with reports being generated to allow for high-end analysis. The application layer's data access control mechanisms are also managed at this layer. Because of its complex and massive computational requirements, this management layer is generally operated on highly potential devices. From the above discussion, it is considered that due to the architecture's simplicity, the five-layered IoT architecture is the most commonly used paradigm for several IoT applications.

2.2   Understanding the Basic Concepts of Artificial Intelligence

2.2.1   Introduction to AI

AI is concerned with the design of intelligence. If fact, it is actually concerned with the design of intelligence in artificial artifacts and artificial devices. Thus, artificial systems or man-made systems are building intelligence into them. This term was coined by McCarthy in 1956 at the famous Dartmouth conference [2]. Now, the term artificial is easy to understand, but what is intelligence?

It is very difficult to define intelligence. Often, intelligence is perceived as something that characterizes humans. If you take human beings to be intelligent you can say that artificial intelligence means having behavior which is similar to that of a human. In fact, there are two thoughts here. First, is to have a machine or system that behaves like a human. Humans are not always completely intelligent, although they have a good level of intelligence. In fact, although humans are relatively intelligent, they do not always behave intelligently. Second, is the other idea that artificial intelligence is concerned with intelligence which results in the ideal, best, or most rational behavior. It enables a machine to behave in the best possible manner. There is another dichotomy in this definition. When we talk about behavior what sort of behavior are we talking about? There are two main types of behavior that people generally refer to. The first is thinking: thinking intelligently, reasoning properly and intelligently in order to come up with a solution. And the second approach is to talk about not thinking but acting, that is how the system actually acts or behaves. Therefore, we can talk about intelligence as something which characterizes humans or something that means behavior in the best possible manner or behaving rationally.

2.2.2 Approaches to AI

Again, think about intelligence as thought or intelligence in action. Therefore, based on this criterion we can look at the different ways of defining AI. So, we may look at thought processing or reasoning versus behavior, or look at human-like performance versus ideal rational performance. Figure 2.2 shows the four different definitions that emerge from these two dichotomies.

On the one hand, we have thought or reasoning versus behavior and on the other hand we have human-like performance versus ideal performance. Therefore, there are systems that think like humans.

For example, the famous Turing test, which was devised by Alan Turing, in which a system which passed the Turing test would be one that behaves like a human or thinks like a human [3]. The second definition is systems that think rationally. The school of thought including philosophers, mathematicians and computer scientists who have worked on logic and laws of thought adheres in this approach. Third, there are systems that act like humans; cognitive scientists look at the properties of systems that act like humans. Finally we have the definition of systems that act rationally or systems that act in the best possible manner [4]. Now, for this we have the approach of constructing a rational agent, that is an agent which acts rationally. Alan Turing was considered by many to be the father of AI due to his devising of the Turing test.

In the Turing test the following experimental set up is used. There will be a closed room, and in this closed room there will be a being which may be a computer or a human. There is an interrogator outside the room. The

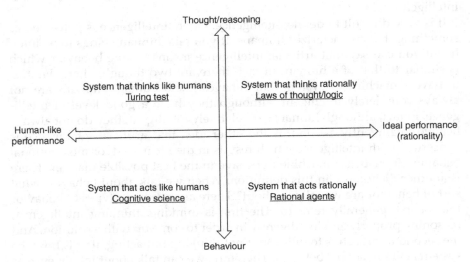

FIGURE 2.2
Different approaches of the AI technique.

interrogator does not know whether the being inside the room is a computer or a human. Therefore, what the interrogator does is asks questions, and the being inside the room processes these questions and returns some answer, with the interrogator in a separate room receiving the answers on a screen.

Now the interrogator has to make out from the answers whether the being inside the room is a computer or human. If there is a computer inside the room then it tries to convince the interrogator that it is actually a human being in the way that it answers the questions, and it is the task of the interrogator to decide whether it is human or not.

If the interrogator cannot reliably distinguish between a human answerer and a computer answerer then we can say that the computer system possesses artificial intelligence. This was the test devised by Turing to discover whether the machine possessed sufficient intelligence to match that of a human in answering questions. Now let us look at problems with AI.

2.2.3 AI Problems

Intelligent entities or agents need to be able to do different types of tasks. There are some tasks which are regular tasks that we do as a matter of fact in our daily life and there are some tasks that we consider intelligent, such as solving difficult mathematical problems, playing games of chess in an expert fashion and other activities which intelligent people can do well.

An example of a routine task is planning routes. Suppose you want to go to a place from the market and you plan a path along which you will go. Or you want to go from a place to, let us a say, a particular place in Delhi and you have to plan the journey and path. Something that could be done is trying to recognize objects or recognize faces of people, which requires vision.

Third, we communicate with each other through natural language. Fourth, we navigate around obstacles on the street. Therefore, these are tasks that we carry out routinely. In fact, most animals carry out these tasks routinely. And then there are expert tasks, such as medical diagnosis, which are only performed by doctors or experts in the field. Mathematical problem solving can be done effectively only by good mathematicians.

Now, which of these problems are easy for a computer to do and which are hard? Surprisingly, it has been much easier to mechanize many of the high-level tasks which are so-called expert tasks, which has been easier in the history of AI and the history of computers. It has proven easier to solve problems which are really the domain of experts, however AI has not had the same success in dealing with mundane tasks.

For example, AI systems can easily carry out symbolic integration. Some of these systems have been able to prove theorems. AI systems also can play chess quite well. There are systems that provide medical diagnoses in particular domains. However, there are some things that humans and animals do quite effortlessly, for example, walking around without running into things, catching prey and avoiding predators, interpreting complex sensory information, modeling the internal states of other animals trying to understand what they are thinking about us, planning what to say and also working as a team or collaborating. These tasks, unfortunately, have not all been easy for machines to perform. Let us look at some of the basic intelligent behaviors in humans:

Perception: Ability to see, hear sensory information;

Reasoning: Reasoning with the information that we have;

Learning: Learning for new situations, understanding natural language, communicating in natural language, solving problems.

Hence these things, namely perception, reasoning, learning, language, understanding and solving problems are examples of some of the things that we want our AI systems to solve. Having looked at the definition of AI, let us discuss some examples of AI systems that have been created.

Some of the applications of AI include the following: computer vision, image recognition including face recognition, robotics, natural language processing and natural language understanding, speech processing, etc. The practical impact of AI is that AI components are embedded in numerous devices.

AI systems are in everyday use in detecting credit card fraud, in configuring products, in complex planning tasks and in advising physicians. Also, intelligent tutoring systems provide an additional benefit of personal attention to the system. These systems are currently being used and have had a tremendous impact because they are so useful.

There is a system called ALVINN, which stands for Autonomous Land Vehicle in a Neural Network [5], which was designed in 1989 by Dean Pomerleau at Carnegie Mellon University. This system drove a car from the east coast to the west coast of the United States of America using computer control. It drove completely autonomously for most of the 2850 miles. Only for 50 miles, especially at exits to freeways, etc., did the human driver take charge. For 2800 miles the car drove itself. The idea behind this car is quite simple. In front of the car is a camera which takes a picture of the road in front. The picture or image is used in a neural network. The picture is captured into an image containing 30/32 pixels. These pixels are fed into a neural network with four hidden units and the output tells the processor which way to turn the wheel and decide the speed, and so on. In 1997 the Deep Blue chess program developed at IBM beat the then-current world chess champion Gary Kasparov. This was the computer Deep Blue and Gary Kasparov after he lost the match accidentally. In a machine translation if we could have immediate translations between people speaking different languages it would be a remarkable feat with very wide ranging economic and cultural implications [6]. In the world today there many different languages and so we may encounter people whose language we do not understand. In India alone there are many languages, with more than 20 official languages, and so it is not possible to learn each of these. Therefore, it not it a great help to humankind if we had a system which could carry out simultaneous machine translations so that we could effortlessly understand one another.

Full machine translation is not yet available, however, there has been quite some progress in the field of machine translation in a small way. For example, according to Reuters Sources, the US military used a simple one-way translation device in Iraq. US forces used the Phraselator to communicate with injured Iraqi prisoners of war, travelers at checkpoints, and for other peacekeeping duties. Carnegie Mellon University has worked on a system called the speechlator for use in doctor–patient interviews. Imagine how difficult it is when a doctor does not understand the language of the patient. Also, when the patient does not understand the language of the doctor they will not be able to communicate their symptoms accurately to the doctor. Therefore, speechlator is used in order to help doctors understand their patients. In space exploration, robotic space probes autonomously monitor their surroundings, make decisions, and act to achieve their goals.

2.2.4 Types of Artificial Intelligence

Now that we have looked at different examples of systems that use AI, we will briefly look at some approaches to AI and to solving AI tasks. One way of looking at AI is as either strong or weak AI. Strong AI aims to build machines that can truly reason and solve problems. Strong AI includes machines that are self-aware and whose overall intellectual ability is indistinguishable from that of a human.

Therefore, strong AI proponents want to develop systems that are completely intelligent and that can do things completely using their own intelligence. Such systems can be human-like, or non-human-like but rational. When AI was conceived in the 1950s and 1960s there was huge optimism about it and there was a prediction that very soon AI systems would be able to overtake humans and be able to everything that a human can do, and carry out tasks much better and faster than humans.

However, such optimism has been ill founded, and this was partly the reason that some people lost faith in AI techniques. However, after over 50 years of research into AI, we are in a position to understand and appreciate the true difficulty of the different problems that AI faces. Weak AI, unlike strong AI, deals with the creation of some AI that cannot truly reason and solve problems but act as if it were intelligent. Therefore, the proponents of weak AI claim that machines which have been suitably programmed can simulate human cognition, appear to behave intelligently, and appear to do tasks well and intelligently without really having the same intelligence or understanding as humans. Therefore, strong AI really deals with machines that have mental states that think, reason, and understand their behavior, whereas weak AI is involved in simulating human behavior or simulating intelligent behavior without really claiming that the reasoning process behind it is intelligent.

The goal of applied AI is to produce viable smart systems. For example, it would be nice to have a security system that is able to recognize the faces of people who are permitted to enter a particular building. There are certain applications which are useful to us that applied AI aims to solve intelligently, not necessarily by constructing a complete intelligent agent but rather an agent which is intelligent in doing a specific task. For example, recognize people, detect credit card fraud, or drive a vehicle autonomously. Therefore, they take up specific tasks and develop systems that solve those tasks. Fourth, cognitive AI deals with the studies where computers are used to test theories about how the human mind works. Cognitive scientists want to understand how humans act, behave, and think, and these theories can be tested by building them into machines and watching and testing how well the machines function using those theories.

In the core areas we talk about knowledge representation, reasoning, and machine learning.

General algorithms: search, planning, constraint, satisfaction.

Perception: vision, natural language processing, robotics.

Applications: game playing, AI and education, distributed agents.

Uncertainty: probabilistic approaches, decision theory, reasoning with symbolic data.

What can today's AI systems do? We have systems that can recognize faces, we have almost autonomous vehicles, and our natural language processing systems can do simple machine translations. Our expert systems can carry out medical diagnosis in a narrow domain. In learning, our text categorization systems can work and categorize the text from about thousand topics. In games, AI systems have achieved grand master level in chess where in the noisy world we have good champion programmers who are playing checkers at every level.

However, there remain many limitations to what AI can do. AI systems currently cannot understand natural language robustly. AI systems cannot yet surf the web or interpret an arbitrary visual scene. We have seen that they can recognize facial images or work in a narrow domain of recognition. AI systems cannot fully learn a natural language. They cannot construct plans in all sorts of dynamic real-time domains in general.

2.2.5 Limitations of Artificial Intelligence

When thinking about the limitations of AI, the first thing that comes to mind is data. AI runs on data, however, data can be imperfect, so if the data are unreliable for the input, the algorithm and results are also affected. Data can be biased, inaccurate or may not be truly representative of the data set that it is supposed to be. These are very important considerations to think about. Data are seen by some as the new oil of the 21st century and they have to be clean and accurate because, if you think about the value of data, it requires taking the data and breaking it down, analyzing it and then using that information. If that information to start with is not clean or reliable then there is no value in the output that results.

A global study has been done to establish ethical guidelines across the globe looking at corporations as well as governments and other principals involved in AI [7]. They found that there was no unified database, and they came up with five key areas of ethics as a solid framework in which to discuss the considerations or limitations of AI.

Transparency: The communication and disclosure about the information that is being collected and used in an AI program.

Justice, Fairness and Equity: The biases in the algorithm, even if the data are clean for creating the algorithm. Biases will be there and so we cannot assume that an algorithm is impartial.

Nonmaleficence: There is the intentional misuse of the data, For example, cyber warfare and malicious hacking.

Responsibility: Who is responsible? There is a lot of talk about responsible AI but it is really defined by AI developers, designers and institutions, and the AI industry as a whole.

Privacy: We have a right to uphold and protect our data, so data security and data protection are other considerations in AI. Although the human element is missing, this is an obvious part of the limitations of AI.

The adoption of AI in education varies. Research into the effectiveness of AI in education is emergent. Currently, it is a moving target, so there's also a fear that it is curriculum driven and not driven jointly with students. Hence, student agency is another limitation, and for AI that student agency is not necessarily propagated. Using AI in education and the roles of teachers are changing. Thus, is not an easy thing to adopt, which is another reason that the adoption of AI is somewhat varied.

2.3 Layered Architecture of Blockchain Technology

Blockchain has significant impacts on finance, cryptocurrencies and socio-economic activities. It is an ensembled innovative technology that combines

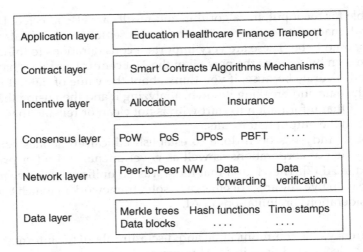

FIGURE 2.3
Layered architecture of blockchain technology.

economics, cryptography and computer science. A six-layered reference architecture is proposed that describes the major components of the blockchain system, as shown in Figure 2.3.

2.3.1 Data Layer

The key techniques are provided in the data layer to manipulate heterogeneous data gathered from physical, cyber and social spaces [8–10].

The data are packed into chained blocks, which are maintained in all participating nodes of the blockchain network by exploiting the data structure of hashed, asymmetrically encrypted and Merkle trees. Particularly, the node which has won in the consensus competition is influenced to package the data created within a certain period of time. The generated new block, along with the time-stamp, denotes the creating time of the competition. If any conflict occurs due to double spending, only one version or a majority of nodes would be chosen and added to the existing blocks. As depicted in Figure 2.4, a Bitcoin block comprises a header that includes the meta-information about the block and the body part contains a Merkle tree structure of hashed data. The blocks are organized in chronological order that contains the complete history of block generation. In the data layer, time stamp and Merkle tree are considered as the two significant components of the blockchain ledger. The inclusion of the timestamp facilitates the precise positioning and traceability of blockchain data. The Merkle tree assists in realizing efficient, rapid and secured verification of blockchain data. Moreover, blockchain is likely to be

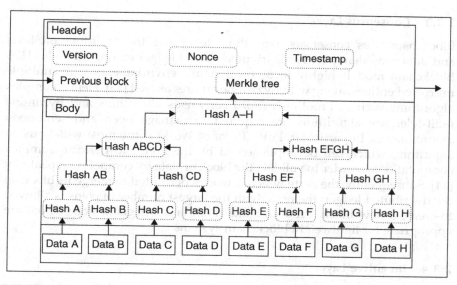

FIGURE 2.4

Block details based on the Merkle tree structure.

extensively used in several time-sensitive scenarios. The timestamp endows blockchain data with being persistently available and paves a way to search out the historical data also.

2.3.2 Network Layer

The network layer focuses on decentralized communication models and their related mechanisms such as data forwarding, verification and distributed networking. Most blockchain applications deal with a dynamic environment consisting of an enormous number of connected devices. The decentralized environment in blockchain can be topologically configured as P2P networks. All participating nodes in the blockchain network are impartially privileged without any middle-man intervention, hence the blockchain system entails bottom-up control and is decentralized. The nodes track the network activities and verify the broadcasted blocks by maintaining a built-in checklist. The decision is made by forwarding the valid blocks to the neighboring nodes and by discarding the invalid nodes. Finally, the blocks agree by the majority of nodes that are added onto the blockchain. The P2P decentralized network supports blockchain as a potential architecture for the future generation of cloud computing. A cloud model evolved with many centralized servers acts as a decentralized model, which facilitates interaction and communication among decentralized entities [11].

2.3.3 Consensus Layer

Blockchain uses consensus algorithms to ensure the fault-tolerant level and data consistency of the distributed shared ledger among all nodes [12]. Blockchain models highly focus on dynamic environments with multiple untrusted entities, along with Byzantine failures as well [13]. Hence, complex algorithms such as Proof-of-X (PoX) consensus algorithms and Byzantine fault-tolerance algorithms are required to manage open and semi-open environments. In particular, PoW (Proof-of-Work) is the most widely using algorithm, which can be implemented by the nodes to perform complex computations in order to validate the block or data by competing repeatedly [14]. Subsequently, the node which is won is permitted to merge its block on the distributed ledger; the node with the largest number of coins is allowed to create a new block. Proof-of-Stake (PoS) and delegated PoS (DPoS) are appropriate for lightweight blockchain systems.

2.3.4 Incentive Layer

In the incentive layer, economic rewards are introduced to maximize the revenue by guaranteeing the trusted ecosystem in the blockchain network. The block creation and data verification processes are considered as the crowdsourcing task for the participating nodes by contributing the computing power. Such nodes are self-motivated agents, and the incentive-based compatible mechanisms are required to satisfy the individual node requirements. In cryptocurrencies, once a block is created, cryptocurrencies are issued as a reward to the node which has won in order to motivate the participating nodes in the complete network. The incentive layer acts as a driving force, particularly in public blockchains. It leverages blockchain by supporting micropayments in real time, establishing cryptocurrency-based financial trading in blockchain. It is optional for private blockchains that are partially centralized for closed and semi-open scenarios. In fact, trusted entities can participate without any financial requirements.

2.3.5 Contract Layer

Various mechanisms and algorithms (e.g., smart contract) are exploited to trigger the static data, assets or money, and they provides an abstract view of business logics in the blockchain systems. Smart contracts are well-defined as a set of self-enforcing, self-executing and self-verifying rules stored and maintained by the blockchain. Once the set of parties has agreed with the predefined rules, the codifying process could be initiated with the smart contract by cryptographically signing it and disseminating it in the P2P network. The verified smart contract will be appended to the distributed ledger. Once the preconditions are activated, the corresponding actions are carried out without any human intervention, as depicted in Figure 2.5. This transforms

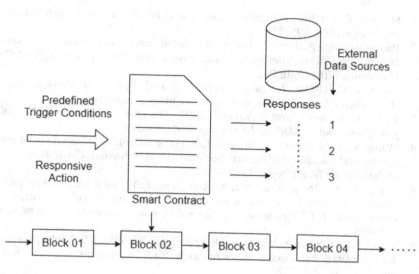

FIGURE 2.5
Smart contract in blockchain.

the digital assets in the form of smart features that could be managed in an automatic manner, thus reducing the complexity and increasing programmability and autonomy [15].

2.3.6 Application Layer

This layer deals with several use-cases and applications of blockchain, since the technology has now gained tremendous attention in different industrial sectors. Blockchain has reshaped the traditional applications with its characteristics such as disintermediated, decentralized systems, by attracting many investors and startup companies.

References

1. Sumathi, D., and T. Poongodi (2020). Internet of Things: From the foundations to the latest frontiers in research, *IoT Network Architecture and Design, De-Gruyter, Internet of Things*, 63.
2. Moor, J. (2006). The Dartmouth College artificial intelligence conference: The next fifty years. *Ai Magazine*, 27(4), 87–89.
3. Schoenick, C., P. Clark, O. Tafjord, P. Turney, and O. Etzioni (2017). Moving beyond the turing test with the Allen AI science challenge. *Communications of the ACM*, 60(9), 60–64.

4. Skinner, B. F. (1985). Cognitive science and behaviourism. *British Journal of psychology*, 76(3), 291–301.
5. Pomerleau, D. A. (1989). *Alvinn: An Autonomous Land Vehicle in a Neural Network*. Artificial Intelligence and Psychology Project, Carnegie-Mellon University, Pittsburgh, PA.
6. Sager, J. C. (1994). *Language Engineering and Translation: Consequences of Automation* (Vol. 1). John Benjamins Publishing, Amsterdam.
7. Jobin, A., M. Ienca, and E. Vayena (2019). The global landscape of AI ethics guidelines. *Nature Machine Intelligence*, 1(9), 389–399.
8. Wang, X., L. Li, Y. Yuan, P. Ye, and F. Y. Wang (2016). ACP-based social computing and parallel intelligence: Societies 5.0 and beyond. *CAAI Transactions on Intelligence Technology*, 1(4), 377–393.
9. Wang, X., X. Zheng, X. Zhang, K. Zeng, and F. Y. Wang (2016). Analysis of cyber interactive behaviors using artificial community and computational experiments. *IEEE Transactions on Systems, Man, and Cybernetics: Systems*, 47(6), 995–1006.
10. Wang, F. Y., Y. Yuan, X. Wang, and R. Qin (2018). Societies 5.0: A new paradigm for computational social systems research. *IEEE Transactions on Computational Social Systems*, 5(1), 2–8.
11. Yuan, Y., and F. Y. Wang (2016). Blockchain: The state of the art and future trends. *Acta Automatica Sinica*, 42(4), 481–494.
12. Chen, C. P., G. X. Wen, Y. J. Liu, and F. Y. Wang (2014). Adaptive consensus control for a class of nonlinear multiagent time-delay systems using neural networks. *IEEE Transactions on Neural Networks and Learning Systems*, 25(6), 1217–1226.
13. Fan, J., L. T. Yi, and J. W. Shu (2013). Research on the technologies of Byzantine system. *Journal of Software*, 24(6), 1346–1360.
14. Kraft, D. (2016). Difficulty control for blockchain-based consensus systems. *Peer-to-Peer Networking and Applications*, 9(2), 397–413.
15. Wang, F. Y., Y. Yuan, C. Rong, and J. J. Zhang (2018). Parallel blockchain: An architecture for CPSS-based smart societies. *IEEE Transactions on Computational Social Systems*, 5(2), 303–310.

3

Artificial Intelligence Enabling IoT Optimization

The emergence of artificial intelligence (AI) has changed the entire ecosystem of the world to a triggered environment and reduced the need for human intervention and effort. The Internet of Thigs (IoT) has evolved different performance evolutions through various other computing networks. The development incorporated with cloud computing is called fog computing, which is the extended version of cloud computing created by CISCO for real-time communication and extended bandwidth usage for IoT devices and increasing operational efficiency [1]. Fog computing also refers to edge computing, which uses real-time data processing and a cloud environment with greater speed [2].

This processing involves distributed processing rather than centralized control—the self-driving vehicle is a prominent example which works with AI technology in a distributed nature. AI plays a vital role in the clinical and health industries with systematic support for IoT-equipped devices. The rapid development of cardiovascular and oncology specializations with AI-powered technological has had a significant impact on the medical industry.

The IoT market is advancing almost daily. This includes the IoT, which integrates things with multiple industrial machineries, manufacturing plants and medical and computational transitional systems. Different factors have made sophisticated changes to IoT industries; one of the most prominent roles is the edge computing system. The current cloud computing system has failures in regard to security and privacy issues for IoT devices. These concerns about security resulted in the introduction of edge technology. IoT's three main essential components are devices we call things, the cloud services used and intelligence for action [3] (see Figure 3.1).

The introduction of AWS IoT services (see Figure 3.2) created more configuration and security for the devices in the cloud environment. The interoperability of Amazon services and IoT devices was enabled by these AWS IoT services. The real-time network connection termination is a common problem, therefore devices that can be working with an offline mode can be supported by the repository services of AWS IoT services. Another property of AWs services is that the new version for updated data can be made as a different version; sometimes, a new model may be incompatible with the older version, so there is provision to switch back to the old model [2]. The

DOI: 10.1201/9781003046462-4

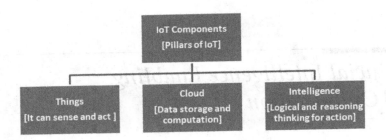

FIGURE 3.1
Basic components of the IoT.

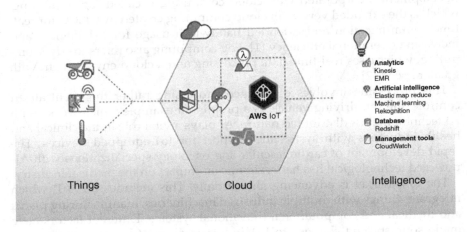

FIGURE 3.2
AWS IoT service.

AWS IoT services involve intelligence that corresponds to electronic medical records, redshift databases and cloud watches for management tools and services.

There are many edge computing platforms used with IoT services such as AWS Green Grass, Azure IoT Edge, Google cloud IoT Edge, etc. [2]. The cloud uses globally available data and resources. In contrast, edge is an intelligence offloaded from the cloud to IoT devices. The edge mechanism is an intermediator between the cloud and IoT devices. As it comes with AI, edge services have become a destination for running machine learning and artificial intelligence processing.

Edge computing distributes the cloud services and makes them available to all devices, reducing the latency time. It moves the core cloud services to actual data, strengthening the public cloud platform by introducing security and privacy services. The edge service the data are serviced locally and delivered at network services. Edge services reduce the round trip for passing data to the cloud.

The AWS core part connects devices to the cloud. Each device should be connected to the IoT core, and before that, it should be registered to this core, and it will certify devices with the digital identity for the particular device. The AWS IoT core has a workflow as shown in Figure 3.3 [4].

The initial aspect is authentication and authorization. It moves to the device gateway, cloud endpoint and the message broker for feeding devices to cloud-like metadata and commands. The subsequent flow is the rules engine that is used to describe how messages will arrive and flow into the cloud. The next part is the device shadow which is the digital identity of the physical device running, and all the changes news first reach the device shadow and then propagate to the corresponding devices. The device shadow acts as a buffer between the current and next state of the devices. The last part is the device registry extensive database connected to devices, cloud and services.

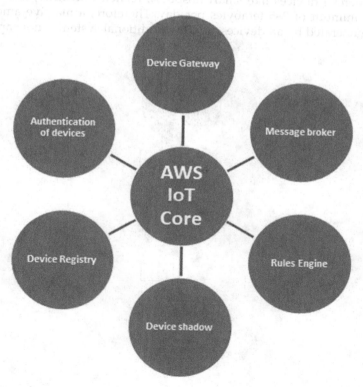

FIGURE 3.3
AWS IoT core.

3.1 Implementation of Edge Mechanism through Artificial Intelligence

Edge computing can be implemented through artificial intelligence by allocating the resources intelligently and accurately. The computational complexity and delay in the communication were the major drawbacks of the traditional system. Still, the development of edge computing with artificial intelligence mastered this problem. The emergence of edge computing solves computing power and data gathering issues in a highly reliable and faster way. Therefore, edge computing has pushed the cloud services to the edge of the network and gathers data to make a local decision more quickly. The Internet of Things creates a provision for edge computing to use commercial objects with perfect decision-making using machine learning algorithms. The edge implementation mechanism reduces the latency. It also helps devices that are not frequently connected to the Internet and can make intelligent decisions with edge computing backup processing to stabilize network connectivity.

Commercial devices like smart hospitals, related industries, and aircraft use a minimum of 2–5 terabytes per day. Therefore, a massive amount of data is generated by all devices, and the traditional system is not capable of

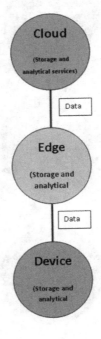

FIGURE 3.4
Distributed nature of edge computing.

adapting to these devices, which has required that edge technology make a drastic change to cloud services. The conventional cloud system focused on storage, computation, and analytics, but edge computing involves a distributed computing approach with localization methods that are data-driven and transmitted through these devices (see Figure 3.4).

The main advantage of edge computing is it ensures the privacy of data. If any user does not want to store data in the cloud but instead to use it locally for current processing, edge computing will assist for the particular session with privileged instructions. Scalability, security and lower cost are other features of edge computing.

The technology that is used for edge computing is AI and machine learning, time-sensitive networking, 5G, etc. Here we are dealing more with artificial intelligence technology, incorporated with machine learning, reflecting tremendous changes in the technological world. As is known, there are open source technologies that will support the feasibility mode for the working of AI technology with a perfect ecosystem for building a real-time intelligent system [4].

3.2 Anomaly Detection of Trained Sensor Data Using the SVM and PCA Mechanism

Anomaly detection is an important research topic in data mining and machine learning. Anomaly detection refers to the problem of finding patterns in data that do not conform to expected behavior. These nonconforming patterns are referred to as anomalies, outliers, discordant observations, exceptions, aberrations, surprises, peculiarities or contaminants in different application domains. Anomaly detection finds extensive use in various applications such as fraud detection for credit cards, insurance or health care, intrusion detection for cybersecurity, fault detection in safety-critical systems and military surveillance of enemy activities [5].

However, most anomaly detection methods are typically implemented in batch mode and cannot be easily extended to large-scale problems without sacrificing computation and memory requirements. The existing methods include normal data with multiclustering structure and data in a higher high-dimensional space. It is typically not easy for the former case to use linear models such as PCA to estimate the data distribution if there are multiple data clusters present. Moreover, many learning algorithms encounter the "curse of dimensionality" problem in a highly high-dimensional space. Although handling high-dimensional data does not need to compute or keep the covariance matrix, PCA might not be preferable in estimating the principal directions for such kinds of data.

This chapter proposes an online oversampling principal component analysis (osPCA) algorithm to address this problem. The OSPCA aims to detect outliers from a large amount of data via an online updating technique. Unlike initial principal component analysis (PCA)-based approaches, the entire data matrix or covariance matrix is not stored. This approach is especially of interest for online or large-scale problems. By oversampling the target instance and extracting the principal direction of the data, osPCA allows us to determine the anomaly of the target instance according to the variation of the resulting dominant eigenvector. Since osPCA needs not explicitly perform eigen analysis, the proposed framework is favored for online applications that have computation or memory limitations.

3.2.1 Principal Component Analysis

Principal component analysis (PCA) is a well-known unsupervised dimension reduction method that determines the data distribution's principal directions. PCA is a well-established technique for dimensionality reduction and multivariate analysis [5]. Examples of its many applications include data compression, image processing, visualization, exploratory data analysis, pattern recognition and time series prediction. The popularity of PCA is due to three essential properties. First, it is the optimal linear scheme for compressing high-dimensional vectors into a set of lower-dimensional vectors and then reconstructing the original location. Second, the model parameters can be computed directly from the data—for example, by diagonalizing the sample covariance matrix. Third, compression and decompression are easy operations to perform given the three model parameters—they require only matrix multiplication. A multidimensional hyperspace is often challenging to visualize [6].

The main objectives of unsupervised learning methods are to reduce dimensionality, scoring all observations based on a composite index and similar clustering comments together based on multivariate attributes. Summarizing multivariate attributes by two or three variables that can display graphically with minimal loss of information is helpful in knowledge discovery. Because it is hard to visualize a multidimensional space, PCA is mainly used to reduce the dimensionality of d multivariate attributes into two or three dimensions. In mathematical terms, PCA is a technique where n correlated random variables are transformed into $d \leq n$ uncorrelated variables. The uncorrelated variables are linear combinations of the original variables and can express the data in a reduced form. Typically, the first principal component of the transformation is the linear combination of the actual variables with enormous variance.

The first principal component is the projection on the direction in which the variance of the projection is maximized. The second principal component is the linear combination of the original variables with the second-largest variance and orthogonal to the first principal component, and so on [6]. In many data sets, the first several principal components contribute most of the variance in the original data set. The rest can be disregarded with minimal loss of the variance for dimension reduction of the data set. PCA has been widely used in the domain of image compression, pattern recognition and intrusion detection. The distance of each observation is measured from the center of the data for anomaly detection. The distance is computed based on the sum of squares of the standardized principal component scores.

To obtain principal directions, one needs to construct the data covariance matrix and calculate its dominant eigenvectors. These eigenvectors will be the most informative among the vectors in the original data space and are considered the principal directions. Let $A = [x1T;x2T; \ldots\ldots xnT] \in IRn \times p$, where each row xi represents a data instance in p dimensional space, and n is the number of the cases. Typically, PCA is formulated as the following optimization problem [5]:

$$\min_{u\in IR^{p\times k}, \|u=I\|} \sum_{i=1}^{n} UU^{T}\left(x_{i}-\overline{\mu}\right)\left(x_{i}-\overline{\mu}\right)^{T} \tag{3.1}$$

U is a matrix consisting of k dominant eigenvectors. From this formulation, one can see that the standard PCA can be viewed as a task of determining a subspace where the projected data have the most significant variation. PCA is formulated as the following optimization problem. One can see that the standard PCA can be viewed as a task of determining a subspace where the projected data have the most significant variation. Alternatively, one can approach the PCA problem by minimizing the data reconstruction error [5–7].

$$\min_{u\in IR^{p\times k}, \|u=I\|} J(U) = \sum_{i=1}^{n} ||(x_{i}-\mu)-(x_{i}-\mu)UU^{T}||2 \tag{3.2}$$

where $(x i - \mu)$ U^{T} determines the optimal coefficients to weigh each principal direction when reconstructing the approximated version of $x i - \mu$. Generally; the problem in either (3.1) or (3.2) can be solved by deriving an eigenvalue decomposition problem of the covariance data matrix,

$$\sum_{A} U = U\Lambda \tag{3.3}$$

where,

$$\sum_{A} \frac{1}{n} \sum_{i=1}^{n} (xi-\mu)(xi-\mu)T \tag{3.4}$$

is the covariance matrix, and μ is the global mean. Each column of U represents an eigenvector of ΣA, and the corresponding diagonal entry in Λ is the associated eigenvalue. For dimension reduction, the last few eigenvectors will be discarded due to their negligible contribution to the data distribution.

While PCA requires the calculation of the global mean and data covariance matrix, it was found that both are sensitive to the presence of outliers, if there are outliers present in the data, dominant eigenvectors produced by PCA will be remarkably affected by them, and thus this will cause a significant variation of the resulting principal directions.

3.2.2 The Use of PCA for Anomaly Detection

The variation of principal directions when removing or adding a data instance is discussed here, including how to utilize this property to determine the outliers of the target data point [5].

Figure 3.5 illustrates the effect of adding/removing an outlier or standard data on principal directions. The clustered blue circles in Figure 3.5 represent regular data instances, the red square denotes an outlier, and the green arrow is the dominant principal direction. From Figure 3.5, the principal focus deviates when an outlier instance is added. More specifically, the presence of such an outlier instance produces a large angle between the resulting and the

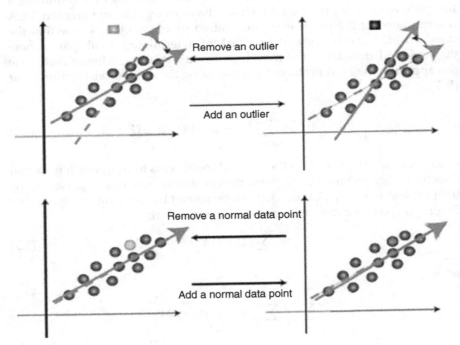

FIGURE 3.5
Effect of adding/removing an outlier or normal data on principal directions.

original principal directions. On the other hand, this angle will be negligible when a specific data point is added. Therefore, this property determines the outlines of the target data point using the LOO strategy.

PCA and the LOO strategy for anomaly detection are combined. Given a data set A with n data instances, extract the dominant principal direction u from it. If the target instance is xt, next compute the leading principal direction ut without xt present. To identify the outliers in a data set, repeat this procedure n times with the LOO strategy.

$$\sum_{\bar{A}} \tilde{u}_t = \tilde{u}_t \lambda \qquad (3.5)$$

where $\bar{A} = A \setminus \{x_t\}$. Note that $\bar{\mu}$ is the mean of $\bar{A}$, and thus

$$\sum_{\bar{A}} = \frac{1}{n-1} \sum_{x_i \in A / \{x_t\}} \left(x_i - \bar{\mu}\right)\left(x_i - \bar{\mu}\right)^T \qquad (3.6)$$

Once these eigenvectors $\tilde{u}_t$ are obtained, use the absolute value of cosine similarity to measure the variation of the principal directions, i.e.

$$s_t = 1 - \frac{\left|\langle \tilde{u}_t, u \rangle\right|}{\left\|\tilde{u}_t\right\|\left\|u\right\|} \qquad (3.7)$$

This set can be considered as a "score of outliers," which indicates the anomaly of the target instance xt. st can also be viewed as the influence of the target instance in the resulting principal direction, and a higher st score (closer to 1) means that the target instance is more likely to be an outlier. If its st is above some threshold for a target instance, identify it as an outlier. This process is a decremental PCA with an LOO scheme for anomaly detection.

Decremental PCA with the LOO strategy considers adding/duplicating a data instance of interest when applying PCA for outlier detection. This setting is convenient for streaming data anomaly detection problems. To be more precise, when receiving a new target instance xt, solve the following PCA problem

$$\sum_{\bar{A}} \tilde{u}_t = \tilde{u}_t \lambda \qquad (3.8)$$

where $\bar{A} = A \cup \{x_t\}$. Note that $\bar{\mu}$ is the mean of $\bar{A}$, and the covariance matrix can be calculated as

$$\sum_{\bar{A}} = \frac{1}{n+1} \sum_{x_i \in A} \left(x_i - \bar{\mu}\right)\left(x_i - \bar{\mu}\right)^T + \frac{1}{n+1}\left(x_i - \bar{\mu}\right)\left(x_i - \bar{\mu}\right)^T \qquad (3.9)$$

After deriving the principal direction, calculate the score st, and the outliers of that target instance can be determined accordingly. This strategy is also preferable for online anomaly detection applications, in which there is a need to determine whether a newly received data instance is an outlier. If the recently acquired data points are standard, adding such models will not significantly affect the principal directions. While one might argue that it might not be sufficient to use the variation of the principal direction to evaluate the anomaly of the data, oversampling PCA alleviates this problem and makes the online anomaly detection problem solvable. It is worth noting that if an outlier is far away from the data cloud (regular data instance) but along the direction of its dominant eigenvector so that this method will not identify such an anomaly. It is also worth pointing out that such an outlier indicates the anomaly in most (if not all) of the feature attributes. This means that most of the feature attributes of this instance are way beyond the normal range/distribution (in the same scale) of each feature variable. As a result, the anomaly of such a data input can be easily detected by simple outlier detection methods such as single-feature variable thresholding. For example, one can calculate the mean and standard deviations of the normal data instances projected onto the dominant eigenvector. For an input data point, if its projected coefficient onto this eigenvector is beyond two or three times the standard deviation, it will be flagged as an outlier. An outlier instance might not be presented in practical outlier detection scenarios due to the violation of system limitations. Taking network traffic/behavior anomaly detection as an example, one might consider power, bandwidth, capacity (data rates) and other parameters of a router/switch as the features to be observed. If a data instance is far away from the normal data cloud but along its principal direction, most of these router parameters simultaneously are above their normal ranges, while some might even exceed their physical limitations. Therefore, the anomaly of this input will be easily detected by system designs and does not require a more advanced outlier detection method.

3.2.3 Oversampling PCA for Anomaly Detection

For practical anomaly detection problems, the size of the data set is typically large. Thus it might not be easy to observe the variation of principal directions caused by the presence of a single outlier. Furthermore, in the above PCA framework for anomaly detection, performing a PCA analysis for a data set with n data instances in a p-dimensional space is not computationally feasible for large-scale and online problems.

When the size of the data set is large, adding (or removing) a single outlier instance will not significantly affect the resulting principal direction of the data. Therefore, advance the oversampling strategy and present an oversampling PCA (osPCA) algorithm for significant scale anomaly detection problems. The proposed osPCA scheme will duplicate the target instance multiple times, and the idea is to amplify the effect of an outlier

rather than that of standard data. While it might not be sufficient to perform anomaly detection based on the most dominant eigenvector and ignore
the remaining ones, the online osPCA method aims to efficiently determine
each target instance's anomaly without sacrificing computation memory
efficiency. More specifically, if the target instance is an outlier, this oversampling scheme allows us to overemphasize its effect on the most dominant
eigenvector and thus focus on extracting and approximating the prevailing
principal direction in an online fashion instead of calculating multiple
eigenvectors carefully.

Suppose that we oversample the target instance $\tilde{n}$ times, the associated
PCA can be formulated as follows

$$\sum_{\overline{A}} \breve{u}_t = \lambda \breve{u}_t \tag{3.10}$$

where $\overline{A} = A \, U\{x_t........x_t\} \in IR^{(n+\tilde{n}) \times p}$. Note that $\overline{\mu}$ is the mean of $\overline{A}$, and the
covariance matrix can be calculated as

$$\sum_{\overline{A}} = \frac{1}{n+\tilde{n}} \sum_{x_i \in A} x_i x_i^T + \frac{1}{n+\tilde{n}} \sum_{i=1}^{\tilde{n}} x_t x_t^T - \breve{\mu} \breve{\mu}^T \tag{3.11}$$

$$= \frac{1}{1+r} \frac{AA^T}{n} + \frac{r}{1+r} x_t x_t^T + \breve{\mu} \breve{\mu}^T \tag{3.12}$$

In this osPCA framework, duplicate the target instance n times (e.g., 10 per
cent of the size of the original data set), and compute the score of outliers st
of that target instance. If this score is above some predetermined threshold,
consider this instance as an outlier. With this oversampling strategy, if the
target instance is normal data, we can observe negligible changes in the
principal directions and the mean of the data. The case of oversampling
an abnormal instance is shown in Figure 3.6. It is worth noting that osPCA
not only determines outliers from the existing data but can also be applied
to anomaly detection problems with streaming data or those with online
requirements.

The using the proposed osPCA for anomaly detection, the oversampling
ratio r will be the parameter for the user to be determined. Since there is
no training or validation data for practical anomaly detection problems, one
cannot perform cross-validation or similar strategies to assess this parameter
in advance. When applying osPCA to detect the presence of outliers, calculating the principal direction of the updated data matrix (with oversampled
data introduced) can be considered the task of eigenvalue decomposition of
the perturbed covariance matrix. Theoretically, the degree of perturbation is
dependent on the oversampling ratio r, and the sensitivity of deriving the
associated dominant eigenvector can be studied as follows:

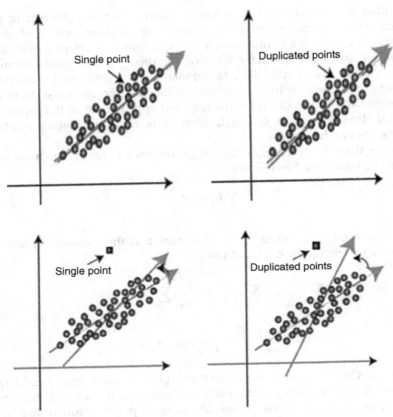

FIGURE 3.6
Effect of an oversampled normal data or outlier instance on the principal direction.

To discuss such perturbation effects, let $A = A = [x_1^T; x_2^T; \ldots x_n^T]$ $\in \mathbb{R}^{n \times p}$ as the data matrix, where each row represents a data instance in a p-dimensional space, and n is the number of the instances. For a target instance x_t oversampled $\tilde{n}$ times, the resulting covariance matrix is derived. Let $\epsilon = \dfrac{\tilde{n}}{n + \tilde{n}}$, calculate the perturbed data covariance matrix Σ_ϵ as

$$\Sigma_\epsilon = \frac{1}{n + \tilde{n}} \left\{ \sum_{i=1}^{n} (x_i - \mu_\epsilon)(x_i - \mu_\epsilon)^T + \right.$$

$$\left. \sum_{i=1}^{\tilde{n}} (x_t - \mu_\epsilon)(x_t - \mu_\epsilon)^T \right\} = \frac{1}{n + \tilde{n}} \left\{ \sum_{i=1}^{n} (x_i - \mu)(x_i - \mu)^T + \right.$$

$$\sum_{i=1}^{\tilde{n}} (x_t - \mu)(x_t - \mu)^T \Big\} + O(\epsilon^2)$$

$$= (1-\epsilon)\Sigma + \epsilon\,\Sigma_{x_t} + O(\epsilon^2) \tag{3.13}$$

Based on (3.13), observe that a normal data instance would make $\epsilon \to 0$ and $\|\Sigma_{x_t}\| \to 0$ and thus the perturbed covariance matrix Σ_ϵ will not be remarkably different from the original Σ. On the other hand, if an outlier instance is a target input to be oversampled, Σ_ϵ will be significantly affected by Σ_{x_t}, and thus the derived principal direction will also be remarkably different from the one without noteworthy perturbation.

The above theoretical analysis supports the use of the variation of the dominant eigenvector for anomaly detection. Using (3.13), while theoretically estimating the perturbed eigenvector $u\epsilon$ with a residual for an oversampled n target instance, such an estimation is associated with the residual term O (ϵ2) and ϵ is a function of n (and thus a function of the oversampling ratio r). Based on (3.13), while larger r values will more significantly affect the resulting principal direction, the presence of the residual term prevents us from performing further theoretical evaluation or comparisons (e.g., threshold determination). Nevertheless, one can expect to detect an outlier instance using the above strategy. No matter how much larger the oversampling ratio r is, the presence of outlier data will affect the dominant eigenvector more than a normal instance. It is found that anomaly detection performance is not sensitive to the choice of the oversampling ratio r.

3.2.4 The Power Method for osPCA

The solution to PCA is determined by solving an eigenvalue decomposition problem. In the LOO scenario, one will need to solve the PCA and calculate the principal directions n times for a data set with n instances. This is very computationally expensive and prohibits the practical use of such a framework for anomaly detection. It can be observed that, in the PCA formulation with the LOO setting, it is unnecessary to recompute the covariance matrices for each PCA. When duplicating a data point of interest, one can easily determine the difference between the updated covariance matrix and the original.

Let $Q = \dfrac{AA^T}{n}$ be the outer product matrix and x_t be the target instance (to be oversampled), to update the mean $\tilde{\mu}$ and the covariance matrix

$$\Sigma_A \hat{\mu} = \frac{\mu + r.x_t}{1+r} \tag{3.14}$$

and

$$\sum_{\tilde{A}} = \frac{1}{1+r}Q + \frac{r}{1+r}x_t x_t^T + \hat{\mu}\mu^T \qquad (3.15)$$

where $r < 1$ is the parameter controlling the size when oversampling x_t. Here one only needs to keep the matrix Q, and there is no need to recompute the entire covariance matrix in this LOO framework. Once the updated covariance matrix is obtained, we can obtain the principal directions by solving each matrix's eigenvalue decomposition problem. To alleviate this computation load, apply the well-known power method, which is a simple iterative algorithm that does not compute matrix decomposition. This method starts with an initially normalized vector u0, which could approximate the dominant eigenvector or a nonzero random vector. Next, the new u_{k+1} is updated by

$$u_{k+1} = \frac{\sum_{\tilde{A}} u_k}{\left\| \sum_{\tilde{A}} u_k \right\|} \qquad (3.16)$$

The sequence $\{u_k\}$ converges under the assumption that the dominant eigenvalue of ΣA is markedly more significant than others. The power method only requires matrix multiplications, not decompositions; therefore, using the power method can alleviate the computational cost in calculating the dominant principal direction. To avoid keeping the data covariance matrix $\sum_{\tilde{A}} \in IR^{(p \times p)}$ during the entire updating process, first compute $y = Au_{k-1}$ and then calculate $u_k = y^T A$. As a result, when applying this technique for the power method, there is no need to add and store the covariance matrix. Here, the data matrix A for the matrix-vector multiplication is kept. Moreover, this multiplication needs to be performed for each iteration of the power method.

3.2.5 Least Squares Approximation and Online Updating for osPCA

The matrix update technique and the power method are combined to solve oversampling PCA for outlier detection. However, the primary concern of the power method is that it does not guarantee a fast convergence, even if it uses prior principal directions for its initial solutions. Moreover, the power method still requires the user to keep the entire covariance matrix, which avoids the problems with high-dimensional data or with limited memory resources. PCA can be considered as a problem to minimize the reconstruction error.

$$\min_{u \in IR^{p \times k}, uu^T = I} J(U) = \sum_{i=1}^{n} \left\| \overline{x}_i - \overline{x}_i UU^T \right\| \qquad (3.17)$$

where x_i is $(x_i - \mu)$, U is the matrix consisting of k dominant eigenvectors, and $UU^T x_i$ is the reconstructed version of x_i using the eigenvectors in U.

$$\min_{u \in IR^{p \times k}, uu^T = I} J_{ls}(U) = \sum_{i=1}^{n} \left\| \overline{x_i} - \overline{x_i} UU'^T \right\|^2$$

$$= \sum_{i=1}^{n} \left\| \overline{x_i} - Uy_i \right\|^2 \qquad (3.18)$$

where U' is the approximation of U, and thus $y_i = U'^T\overline{x_i} \in IR^k$ is the approximation of the projected data $U^T xi$ in the lower k dimensional space. Based on this formulation, the reconstruction error has a quadratic form and is a function of U, which can be computed by solving a least squares problem. The trick for this least squares problem is the approximation of $U'^T\overline{x_i}$ by $y_i = U'^T\overline{x_i}$. In an online setting approximate each $U_i^T\overline{x_i}$ by its previous solution $U_{i-1}^T \overline{x_i}$ as follows

$$\min_{u_t \in IR^{p \times k}, uu^T = I} J_{ls}(U_t) = \sum_{i=1}^{t} \left\| \overline{x_i} - u_i y_i \right\|^2 \qquad (3.19)$$

Where $y_i = U_{i-1}^T \overline{x_i}$. This projection approximation provides a fast calculation of principal directions in oversampling PCA. Linking this least squares form to an online oversampling strategy, then

$$\min_{u_t \in IR^{p \times k}, uu^T = I} J_{ls}(U_t) = \sum_{i=1}^{n} \left\| \overline{x_i} - \widetilde{u_i} y_i \right\|^2 + \left\| \overline{x_t} - \widetilde{u_i} y_t \right\|^2 \qquad (3.20)$$

y_i and y_t are approximated by $U^T\overline{x_i}$ and $U^T\overline{x_t}$, respectively, where U is the solution to the original PCA, and $\overline{x_t}$ is the target instance. When oversampling the target instance $\widetilde{n}$ times, approximate the solution $\widetilde{U}$ by solving the following optimization problem

$$\min_{u_t \in IR^{p \times k}, uu^T = I} J_{ls}(\check{U}) \sim \beta \left(\sum_{i=1}^{n} \left\| \overline{x_i} - \check{U}y_i \right\|^2 \right) + \left\| \widetilde{n}\overline{x_i} - \check{U}y_i \right\|^2 \qquad (3.21)$$

Equivalently, convert the above problem into the following form:

$$\min_{u_t \in IR^{p \times k}, uu^T = I} J_{ls}(\check{U}) \sim \beta \left(\sum_{i=1}^{n} \left\| \overline{x_i} - \check{U}y_i \right\|^2 \right) + \left\| \overline{x_i} - \check{U}y_i \right\|^2 \qquad (3.22)$$

where β can be regarded as a weighting factor to suppress the information n from existing data. Note that the relation between β and the oversampled number $\widetilde{n}$ is $\beta = 1/\widetilde{n} = 1/nr$ where r is the ratio of the oversampled number over the size of the original data set. To improve the convergence rate, use the solution to the original PCA (without oversampling data) as the initial projection matrix. If only the dominant principal direction is of concern, calculate the solution of ~u by taking the derivative with respect to u, and thus have

$$\breve{U} = \frac{\beta\left(\sum_{i=1}^{n} y_i \overline{x}_i\right) + y_t \overline{x}_t}{\beta\left(\sum_{i=1}^{n} y_i^2\right) + y_t^2} \qquad (3.23)$$

This provides an effective and efficient updating technique for osPCA, which allows us to determine the principal direction of the data. This updating process makes anomaly detection in online or streaming data settings feasible. More importantly, since there is only the need to calculate the solution to the original PCA offline, we do not need to keep the entire covariance or outer matrix in the whole updating process.

Once the final principal direction is determined, use the cosine similarity to determine the difference between the current solution and the original one (without oversampling), and thus the score of outlierness for the target instance can be determined accordingly. The pseudocode of online osPCA with the LOO strategy for outlier detection is described in Algorithm 1.

Algorithm 1. Anomaly Detection via Online Oversampling PCA

Require: The data matrix $A = \left[x_1^T; x_2^T \ldots \ldots \ldots; x_n^T\right]$ and the weight β.

Ensure: Score of outliers, $s = [s_1 s_2 \ldots \ldots s_n]$, if s_i is higher than a threshold, x_i is an outlier.

Compute first principal direction U

Keep $\overline{x}_{proj} = \sum_{j=1}^{n} y_j \overline{x}_j$ and $y = \sum_{j=1}^{n} y_j^2$

For $i = 1$ to n do

$$\breve{U} < -\frac{\beta\left(\sum_{i=1}^{n} y_i \overline{x}_i\right) + y_t \overline{x}_t}{\beta\left(\sum_{i=1}^{n} y_i^2\right) + y_t^2}$$

$$s_t < -1 - \left|\frac{< w, \tilde{w} >}{\|\breve{u}\|\|u\|}\right|$$

end

3.2.6 Online Anomaly Detection for a Practical Scenario

For online anomaly detection applications such as spam mail filtering, one typically designs an initial classifier using the normal training data, and this classifier is updated by the newly received normal or outlier data accordingly; however, in practical scenarios, even the training normal data collected in advance can be contaminated by noise or incorrect data labeling osPCA (Over Sampling Principal Component Analysis) with an online updating technique to reduce the computational and memory costs. PCA with a LOO (Leave One Out) strategy is used to detect the outliers by observing the variations in principal directions. LOO illustrates that removing an abnormal data instance has a more significant effect on principal direction than normal data. The variations of principal direction are determined by using the cosine of similarity. We calculated the score of cosine similarity and took it as the score of outliers, and it was taken as the threshold value. If the new data instance is above the predefined threshold value, it takes it as an outlier, otherwise it is considered to be a normal instance. This is not suitable for significant scale problems, for which osPCA is used. Sampling is the duplication of target instance multiple times; with the idea being to amplify the effect of outliers. osPCA does not support online streaming problems. Therefore, in

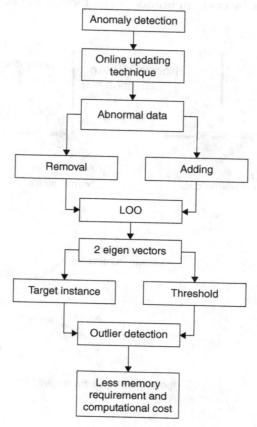

FIGURE 3.7
osPCA with an online updating technique.

the last work osPCA is combined with the online updating technique, which has less computational and memory costs. Figure 3.3 illustrates the osPCA method with the online updating technique.

Data instance is the input. Anomalies are detected by observing the variations in the principal directions. For keeping the variations, LOO is used. If the added item makes significant variations, then it will be considered as an anomaly. Otherwise, it is taken as a normal one. A score of outliers is calculated by finding a cosine of similarity. Two eigenvectors are obtained. One is the target instance, and the other is the threshold. If the added instance is above the threshold, it is considered to be the anomaly. An online updating technique with osPCA (see Figure 3.7) has high computational cost and memory requirements. An online updating osPCA algorithm is used to calculate the dominant eigenvector, while oversampling a target instance is described in Figure 3.6.

The usual and anomalous data received are updated by the classifier. However, in a real-world application, even though the standard data are

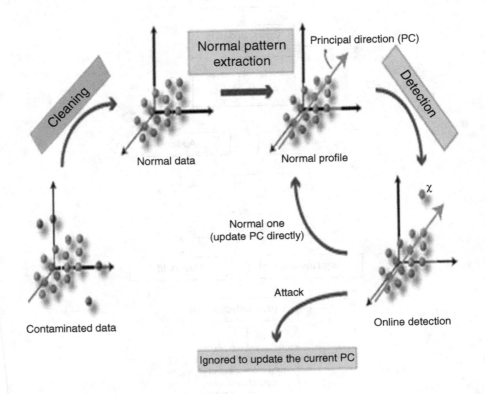

FIGURE 3.8
Framework of online anomaly detection.

collected, they may consist of some noise and wrong labeling of data. To succeed with this approach, one cannot discard these deviated instances online from the usual data. Therefore, the anticipated system architecture of online updating osPCA for outlier detection is shown in Figure 3.8.

This consists of three phases: filtration, clustering and anomaly detection.

3.2.6.1 Filtration

In this detection application, such as spam mail filtering, one typically designs an initial classifier using the standard training data, and this classifier is updated by the newly received normal or outlier data accordingly in practical scenarios; even the training average data collected in advance can be contaminated by noise or incorrect data labeling. To construct a simple yet effective model for online detection, one should disregard these potentially deviated data instances from the training set of standard data.

3.2.6.2 Clustering

The training data are selected only by assumption. Therefore, there is a possibility that some outlier data may be considered standard data in the previous method due to training data. The clustering method is used to solve this problem. The clusters are formed for input data instances, and then the outlier calculation is applied for each cluster to find the outlier exactly. To ensure confidentiality, rigorous security definition and proof of the proposed scheme mechanism is provided. In this, clusters are formed for input data instance, and then the outlier calculation is applied for each cluster to find the outlier exactly.

3.2.6.3 Anomaly Detection

This is used for detecting the outliers of user input. When the user provides information to the system, the system calculates the St Value for the new intake. The new St Value is then compared with the threshold value which was calculated earlier. If the St Value of the new data instance is above the threshold value, then that input data are identified as an outlier, and the system will discard that value. Otherwise, it is considered a standard data instance, and the PCA value of that particular data instance is updated accordingly.

The sequence diagram of the online method is shown in Figure 3.9. Data cleaning is carried out on contaminated data. In this, the instances deflecting the principal direction in large amounts are removed using oversampling principal component analysis. This enables normal data to be secured. Once normal data is obtained, models, i.e. the principal direction, are computed. They are used in analyzing the threshold value for detecting outliers. The most

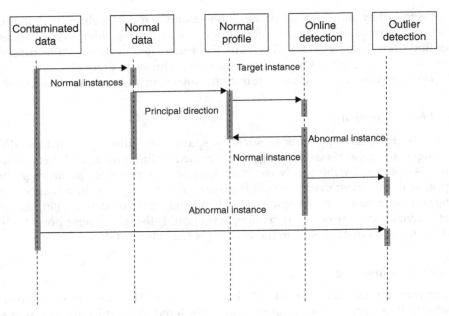

FIGURE 3.9
Sequence diagram of the online method.

miniature score of outliers of the new model is compared with the threshold value. If the most miniature score of outliers is an outlier and ignored to update the current PC. If the instance is standard, i.e., the value of the most miniature score of the outlier is smaller than the defined threshold value, it is detected as a typical instance. This will extract the standard pattern for the remaining most significant outliers compared to the threshold value, then the instance is updated directly to the PC.

3.3 Resilience and Reliability in the IoT through an Intelligence Scheme

Nowadays, the IoT is widely used in network integration through intelligence, recognition technology, pervasive computing and other communication technologies. Therefore, it has been called the world's third wave of information industry development following the computer and the Internet. With the development of IoT technology, its applications are increasingly extending to virtually all areas on an almost daily basis. The most prominent areas are innovative industries, such as smart homes, smart energy, intelligent city, intelligent city healthcare, etc. The IoT is a new technology of Internet access. Through the IoT, objects recognize themselves and obtain intelligent behavior by making or enabling related decisions thanks to the fact that they can communicate information about themselves. These objects can access information that other things have aggregated, or they can add to other services. With the IoT, anything will be able to communicate to the Internet anytime from any place to provide any services through any network to anyone. This creates a new type of application that could involve innovative vehicles and smart homes to offer many benefits such as notifications, security, energy-saving, automation, communication, computers and entertainment.

As the fields of application for IoT are numerous, the IoT security issues are particularly prominent. If IoT suffers network attacks, it may cause various types of damage and even threaten human lives and properties. However, devices in the IoT generate and exchange a massive number of security-critical and privacy-sensitive data, which makes them attractive targets for various attacks. However, existing security solutions are inappropriate. To improve the abilities of monitoring, providing emergency responses, and predicting the development trends of IoT security, a new paradigm called network security situation awareness (NSSA) has been proposed. However, it is limited by its ability to mine and evaluate security situation elements from multisource heterogeneous network security information.

To solve this, the main goal throughout this chapter has been to propose a situation reasoning method based on semantic ontology and user-defined rules for IoT Network Security Situation Awareness (NSSA) from a holistic viewpoint. This method not only realizes the unified and formalized description and the reuse of the heterogeneous network security situation information of the IoT but can also detect the security situation of the network in real time.

The Internet of Things (IoT) has gained significant attention from researchers since it has become an important technology which make ease and intelligence by allowing communication between all objects together with human being. The IoT represents a system that consists of things in the real world and sensors attached to or combined with these things, connected to the internet via a wired and wireless network structure. The IoT sensor can use various types of connections such as RFID, Wi-Fi, Bluetooth and ZigBee, and allows wide area connectivity using many technologies such as GSM, GPRS, 3G, and LTE. IoT-enabled things can share information about the condition of items and the surrounding environment with people, software systems and other machines.

Through the use of IoT technology, humanity will gain in many areas since the IoT will provide a means for intelligent cities, innovative healthcare, smart homes and building, in addition to many critical applications such as intelligent energy, grid transportation, waste management and monitoring.

In this chapter, we review the concept of many IoT applications and future possibilities for new related technologies and the challenges facing implementation of the IoT.

The NSSA model, based on semantic ontology and use-defined rules for IoT security, can perceive the current security situation at all security levels. The reasoning engine can determine the current network security situation based on the ontology model and user-defined rules. Ontology technology can provide a unified and formalized description to solve the semantic heterogeneity in the IoT security domain. Four key subdomains are proposed to reflect the IoT security situation: context, attack, vulnerability, and network flow.

As Figure 3.10 shows, the IoT architecture comprises three layers: the perception layer, network layer and application layer. The perception layer is responsible for collecting basic information through RFID, various sensors, GPS, laser scanners, two-dimensional codes and so on. The network layer is responsible for transmitting information collected by the perception layer to the application layer. The application layer processes the data to meet the needs of users (intelligent transportation, intelligent power, intelligent medical, etc.).

The application layer faces various security issues due to its diverse application types, and technology stands and regulations. Any layer that is attacked will affect the entire system and users. What's more, the security of the network layer and application layer is more critical; hence the IoT requires holistic and real-time security management, which includes real-time attacks and vulnerabilities detection and prediction of a possible attack. However, this security management of the IoT is highly challenging due to heterogeneous devices and the nonuniform data generated by IoT devices. It needs to process and analyze heterogeneous data inputs in real time to make appropriate and sensible decisions. However, existing security solutions are inappropriate as they do not scale to large networks of heterogeneous devices and satisfy real-time detection requirements. To solve these problems, a new

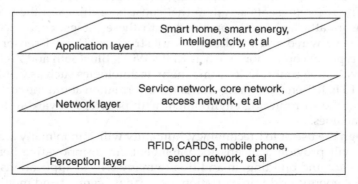

FIGURE 3.10
The architecture of the IoT.

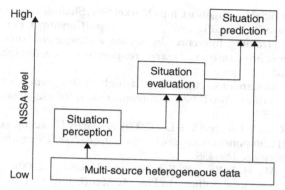

FIGURE 3.11
The conceptual model of NSSA.

network security monitoring technology named network security situation awareness is proposed. If the network security situation awareness technology of the IoT makes a breakthrough, it will play an essential supporting role in IoT security.

3.3.1 Network Security Situation Awareness (NSSA)

The potential safety hazard of IoT exists objectively, and the IoT is more vulnerable to attacks because of the mass of embedded devices and ubiquitous wireless networks. On the one hand, we should enhance the antiattack capability of the IoT; on the other hand, we should also monitor security situations of the IoT in real time and detect threats as early as possible to reduce losses. The challenge of the security situation awareness of the IoT is to mine valuable information from many heterogeneous data generated from sensors and to perceive the current security situation in real time. The proposed concept of NSSA can solve these problems.

The conceptual model of NSSA (Network Security Situation Awareness) is shown in Figure 3.11. This was proposed to improve monitoring, provide an emergency response, and predict the development trend of IoT security. However, it is limited by its ability to mine and evaluate the security situation elements from multisource heterogeneous network security information.

References

1. Mohammed, Zeinab Kamal Aldein, and Elmustafa Sayed Ali Ahmed (2017). Internet of things applications, challenges and related future technologies, *World Scientific News.* 67(2), 126–148, EISSN 2392-2192.

2. Edge Artificial Intelligence Chips Market Size, Share & Trends Analysis Report by Processor (CPU, GPU, ASIC), Device Type (Consumer, Enterprise Devices), Function (Training, Inference), by Region, and Segment Forecasts, 2020–2027.

3. www.freecodecamp.org/learn/responsive-web-design/#basic-html-and-html5

4. https://aws.amazon.com/?sc_channel=EL&sc_campaign=Event_2017_vid&sc_medium=YouTube&sc_content=video1360&sc_detail=SUMMIT&sc_country=US

5. Yeh, Y.-R., Z.-Y. Lee, and Y.-J. Lee (2009). Anomaly Detection via Oversampling Principal Component Analysis. In *Proc. First KES Int'l Symp. Intelligent Decision Technologies*, pp. 449–458.

6. Breunig, M., H.-P. Kriegel, R.T. Ng, and J. Sander (2000). LOF: Identifying density-based local outliers. In *Proc. ACM SIGMOD Int'l Conf. Management of Data*, pp. 440–453.

7. Chandola, V., A. Banerjee, and V. Kumar (2009), Anomaly Detection: A Survey. *ACM Computing Surveys*, 41(3), 15:1–15:58.

4

Transformation of Artificial Intelligence toward Blockchain

The artificial intelligence mechanism involves thinking with intelligence which lacks security enhancements. Artificial intelligence transformed to blockchaining is, in a sense, the formulation of a blockchain mechanism with AI methodology. This mechanism involves an input-processing–computational output system that helps in intelligent contract and human biological thinking.

Cryptocurrencies are the technology built on blockchain to enable a shared distributed tamper-proof ledger to be viewed by anyone with the corresponding software. Unleashing blockchain technology from its application to cryptocurrencies is very important in understanding blockchain technology's broader implications and applications. Differentiating the two will help understand why there is such excitement about blockchain-inspired ruptures. Disruption in bioinformatics, governance, banking, trading, society, politics and even the very structure of the Internet itself is disordered. Generally, blockchain technology will bring disintermediation in everything.

To understand how blockchain technology applications work deeply, it is necessary to understand the logical components of a blockchain ecosystem and the duties of each element. The four main details of any blockchain ecosystem are:

- A node application;
- a shared ledger;
- A consensus algorithm;
- A virtual machine.

4.1 Node Application

Each computer interconnected through the Internet needs to install and run a computer application specific to the ecosystem that it is desired to participate in. for example, using the case of Bitcoin as an ecosystem, each computer must be running the Bitcoin wallet application. In some blockchain applications,

DOI: 10.1201/9781003046462-5

like Bankchain, participation is restricted and requires special permissions to join (referred to as permissioned blockchains). Bankchain only permits banks to run the node application. However, in the Bitcoin ecosystem, anyone can download and install the node application and participate in the ecosystem.

4.2   Shared Ledger

The distributed ledger is a data structure managed inside the node application. Once you have the node application running, you can view the respective ledger (or blockchain) contents for that ecosystem. Interactions are done according to the rules of the ecosystem in which it resides. You can run as many node applications as you like and are permitted to use, and each will participate in its respective blockchain ecosystems. It is important to note that the number of ecosystems you are a participant in doesn't matter as you will only have one shared ledger for each ecosystem.

4.3   Consensus Algorithm

The consensus algorithm is implemented as a portion of the node application by providing the "rules of the game" for how the ecosystem will arrive at a single view of the ledger. Different ecosystems have different methods for attaining consensus depending on the desired features the ecosystem needs. Participation in the consensus-building process, the method for determining the "world state" of the ecosystem, can be vested in several different schemes: proof-of-work, proof-of-stake, proof-of-elapsed-time; each plan qualifies nodes as honest in different ways before participating in the consensus-building process.

4.4   Virtual Machine

A virtual machine represents a machine (real or imaginary) created by a computer program and operated with instructions embodied in a language. It is an abstraction of a device held inside a machine. To some degree, we are already accustomed to the abstraction of real-world objects and entities as virtual objects in a computer. Think of a button in a graphical user interface of an application. You press the button on the screen, and the state of the program inside the computer changes.

4.5 Core Components of Blockchain Architecture

- Node—user or computer within the blockchain architecture (each has an independent copy of the whole blockchain ledger);
- Transaction—smallest building block of a blockchain system (records, information, etc.) that serves as the purpose of blockchain;
- Block—a data structure used for keeping a set of transactions which is distributed to all nodes in the network;
- Chain—a sequence of blocks in a specific order;
- Miners—specific nodes which perform the block verification process before adding anything to the blockchain structure;
- Consensus (consensus protocol)—a set of rules and arrangements to carry out blockchain operations (Figure 4.1).

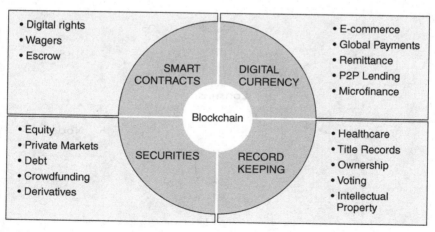

FIGURE 4.1
Blockchain applications.

4.6   Ledger Management

The blockchain is the underlying technology behind applications like Bitcoin. A distributed ledger is essential as it is a list of all events and transactions entered onto it, which is held simultaneously by each node in the network. Whenever a new event or marketing is added to the ledger, encryption is done to everything before it makes the data on the roster become increasingly secure with every addition to the ledger. The ledger is visible to everyone in the network and is secured so that people cannot tamper with it. Every new piece of information added to this ledger is added as a "block." This block is mathematically encrypted and is approved to be added to the ledger according to a series of consensus protocols, that is, ways of supporting additions and protecting against fraud or double-spending without the need for a centralized authority.

A distributed ledger is a decentralized database as it is spread across several different computers or nodes (Figure 4.2). Here every node will maintain the ledger, and if any data changes take place, the ledger will be updated. The updating takes place independently at each node. Through the ledger, along

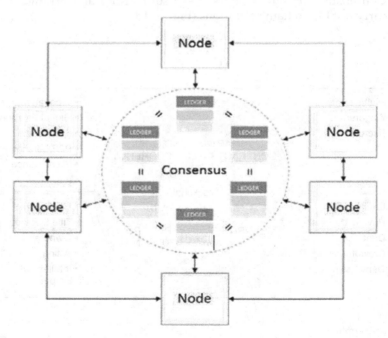

FIGURE 4.2
Ledger management with consensus.

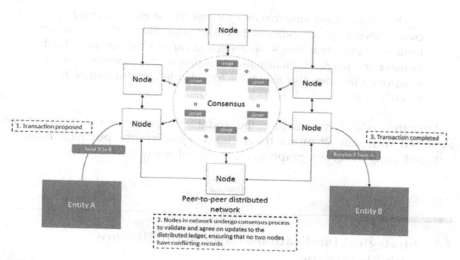

FIGURE 4.3
Ledger management in a distributed network.

with a piece of computer code, you can create "smart contracts." These are a series of clauses that are added to the ledger and powered by computer code. When the clause in the ledger is met, the computer code activates, and the next step of the contract is triggered.

All the nodes are equal in terms of authority. No central authority or server manages the database, which makes the technology transparent. Every node can update the ledger, and other nodes will verify its existence. This property of the distributed ledger makes it an attractive technology for a financial industry or any other industry looking for more transparent technology and those that need a technology that is far from a central authority.

By using distributed ledgers, there is no need for centralized authority. It is a network of ledgers or contracts that is maintained by nodes (Figure 4.3). The nodes can be merged into blocks, making it even easier to support more enormous distributed network ledgers. Even without a central authority, all the information stays secure. To enable the distributed network, technology such as cryptography must assign the data with cryptographic signatures and keys for use. Anything that is stored on the distributed ledger is immutable. Immutability makes it even harder for hackers to try to hack the distributed ledger network such as Bitcoin. Additionally, the absence of the central authority means that it is free from any intentional change.

The following three significant steps involved:

> To initiate a payment, entity A digitally signs a proposed update to the shared ledger with cryptographic tools to transfer funds from its account on the ledger to entity B's account. Upon receiving the transfer request, other nodes authenticate entity A's identity and validate the transaction

by checking to make sure that entity A has the necessary cryptographic credentials to make an update to the record in question. Validation would include, among other things, verifying that entity A has sufficient funds to make the payment. Nodes also take part in the consensus process to agree on the costs that should be included in the next update to the ledger's state.

After the nodes have accepted the update, the properties of the asset are modified such that all future transactions regarding the purchase must be initiated using the cryptographic credentials of entity B.

4.7 Strategical Implication of Swarm Intelligence with Blockchain

Blockchain provides changes to different business perspectives and the economic nature of current technological industries. The existing cryptocurrencies likes Bitcoin and Ethereum are all examples for the corresponding view. To empower the blockchain mechanism the swarm intelligence mechanism is involved with three main algorithms, which is an alternative to the classical algorithms that are as follows:

- Nature-inspired algorithm [evolutionary algorithm (EA)]
- Particle swarm optimization (PSO)
- Ant colony optimization (ACO)

(a) Nature-inspired algorithm [evolutionary algorithm (EA)]
This algorithm is the best solutions for different problems and design strategies in engineering as well as computational methodologies. This algorithm mainly focuses on technological upgradation or revolutionary changes imitating the process of nature or an idea inspired by nature. There are several types of design changes that occurred with the discovery of this algorithm. The following are some of them.

(i) **Aircraft wing design**: This design makes the landing and takeoff of aircraft smoother and controllable, while minimizing drag [3] (see Figure 4.4).

(ii) **Wind turbine design**: The overall performance of the turbine was improved by 40%. This design reduces turbulence across the surface, increasing the angle of attack and decreasing drag. It maximizes and enhances lift devices to control flow over the flipper and maintain lift at a high angle of attack (see Figure 4.5).

 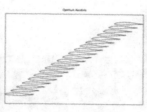 

FIGURE 4.4
Aircraft design from a bird wing.

FIGURE 4.5
Wind turbine design from a humpback whale.

FIGURE 4.6
Bionic car design from a fish-shaped box.

(iii) **Bionic car:** The bionic car makes a feature of fish with hexagon-shaped plates in the door panel which are one-third lighter than the conventional paneling, which makes the car stronger. This shape minimizes drag and maximizes the rigidity of the exoskeleton (see Figure 4.6).

(iv) **Bullet train:** The bullet train included some changes where the train nose was designed after the beak of a kingfisher, which dives smoothly into water, increasing the train speed. This shape minimize micropressure waves [3] (see Figure 4.7).

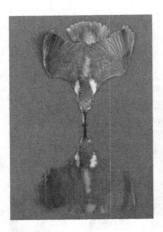

FIGURE 4.7
Bullet train nose from a kingfisher beak.

The above designs take their inspiration from nature, which is a process or methodology of making something as fully perfect, functional or effective as possible, and is thus called optimization. Here we refer to some practical optimization problem characteristics [3]:

- Objective and constraint functions can be nondifferentiable;
- Constraints are nonlinear;
- Discrete/discontinuous search space;
- Mixed variables (integer, real, Boolean, etc.);
- Large number of constraints and variables;
- Objective functions can be multimodal;
- Computationally expensive objection functions and constraints.

Figure 4.8 shows the practical optimization problem characteristics where the decision vectors are the input part that is being changed, and the target output is the objective vector. The input objective in correlation with the corresponding parameters of the simulation model produces a more optimized model [3].

(b) Particle swarm optimization (PSO)

Particle swarm optimization is a population-based stochastic optimization technique developed by Dr Eberhart and Dr Kennedy in 1995 and inspired by the social behavior of birds or a school of fish.

Particle swarm optimization is faster and more economic compared to other optimization techniques. It is a parallel activity and does not

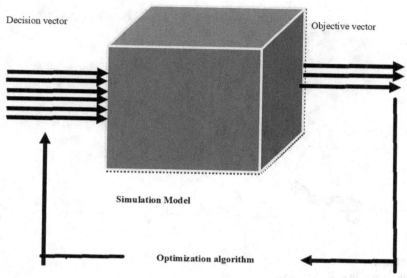

Decision vector

Objective vector

Simulation Model

Optimization algorithm

FIGURE 4.8

Practical optimization problems—characteristics.

use gradient problems. Its main feature is that it does not require the problems to be differentiable. It is very commonly used with the implementation of different tasks and is flexible.

(c) Ant colony optimization (ACO)

Ant colony optimization is a swarm intelligence technique that uses artificial ants as a computational intelligence technique. Ant colony optimization is related to the behavior of some ant species. These ants deposit pheromones on the ground to create a favorable path that should be followed by other members of the colony. Ant colony optimization uses a similar mechanism for solving optimization problems [2].

Ant colony optimization can be used in the traveling salesman problem in which an asset of the city is given and the distance between the cities is well known. The main goal is to find the shortest journey that allows each city to be visited once and only once. The idea is to find a Hamiltonian time of minimal length on a fully connected graph. In ant colony optimization the problems are tackled by simulating several artificial ants moving on a chart that encodes the problem itself. Each vertex represents a city. Each edge represents a connection between two cities. Here, a variable called a pheromone is associated with each edge and it can be read and modified by ants. ACO is an iterative algorithm where at each iteration, several artificial ants are considered. Each of them builds a

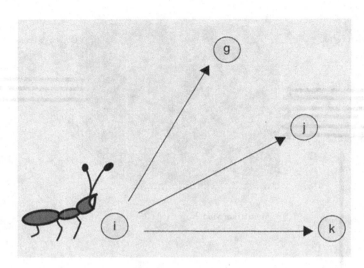

FIGURE 4.9
Artificial ants in a city for ACO.

solution by visiting vertex to vertex in which the primary constraint is visiting the non-visited nodes to be seen. At each iteration the ants use a stochastic mechanism biased by the pheromone: when vertex I is visited then the following vertex is selected stochastically among the previously unvisited one.

In Figure 4.9 an ant is in the city, i chooses the next city to visit via a stochastic mechanism; if j has not been previously seen, it can be selected with a probability that is proportional to the pheromone associated with the edge (i,j)

4.8   Artificial Intelligence-Based Supernode Selection Algorithm

The development of peer-to-peer communication with intercommunication of heterogeneous distributed hash table and proxy SIP is used as a supernode. The election mechanism for selecting the particular supernode is complex, therefore an artificial intelligence scheme is used for this election to simplify it, and the complexity of the computation will be reduced. Here there are different methods used, where the most important are district partition schemes for supernode selection (see Figure 4.10). In this scheme, node

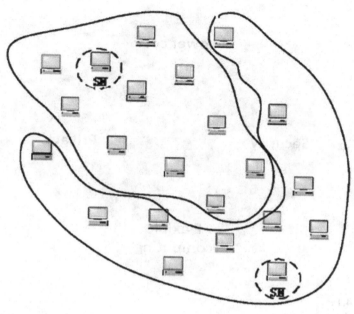

FIGURE 4.10
District partition scheme for supernode selection.

selection is made based on the geographical position and I.P. address and structure of the district hash table.

4.9 Deep Brain—Blockchain Mechanism for Next-Generation Innovation

In artificial intelligence research, memory is considered discretely. This approach is called a deep mind in which the mechanism is that of a neural Turing machine. The linked neural Turing machine will reduce the short-term memory problem of humans by linking the human brain with a neural network [1].

A deep brain is a decentralized artificial intelligence platform that is incorporated with the blockchain mechanism with a higher order of security and privacy, which is generally economical. This mechanism can be traded with the intelligent contact and ledger mechanism. The main features of the deep-brain mechanism are lower cost, security, privacy and flexible computing [1] (see Figure 4.11).

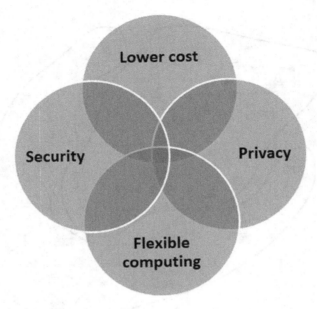

FIGURE 4.11
Features of deep brain.

References

1. www.deepbrainchain.org/
2. Ant_Colony_Optimization.pdf.
3. Thevenot, Axel (2020). *Particle Swarm Optimization (PSO) Visually Explained.* Towards Data Science.

5

Disruptive Technological Aspect of the IoT toward Blockchain

5.1 Introduction

Smartphones are used by many individuals around the world, and their growth is increasing exponentially, along with that of many other gadgets. A few years ago, people were dependent on large desktop computers for solving problems. However, with the steady evolution of microprocessors and embedded devices, the size of computers started to reduce significantly. The most prominent reason for the development of smartphones has been the rise of innovation in the digital revolution. People used a typewriters then replaced it with a personal computers which evolved to a laptop, packet computer, etc.

The applications that are available in smartphones are not quantifiable. They support people in many areas, such as finding the direction to a destination, detecting and notification of any abnormalities in patients, getting a vehicle in case of an emergency, ordering items we require through e-commerce applications. People can even order any food they wish in a few clicks, and also reducing the need to buy books as e-books and e-magazines help to reduce the impact on the environment. The above examples are just a few. They have numerous applications, as these applications can be developed by ordinary individuals to solve real-time problems. This provides a platform for "N" number of opportunities in solving any international issues, which can provide the optimal solution for people at an affordable cost.

Sectors such as agriculture, healthcare, education, transport, military, smart home, industrial Internet are just some of the unlimited areas that they have found uses. The most commonly used operating systems are Android and iOS, accounting for approximately 98% of the total.

DOI: 10.1201/9781003046462-6

5.2 Components of Smart Devices

Smart devices consist of eight major components for performing the desired operations as illustrated in Figure 5.1.

5.2.1 System on Chip

It consists of CPU, GPU, LTE modem, video processor and other functional hardware units and the various System on chip includes Mediatek, Qualcomm, and so on, but all use the same ARM architecture sensors.

The sensors are not limited as they can be updated depending upon the smartphone used., but the most commonly used sensors are gyroscopes, magnetometers, proximity sensors and light sensors.

5.2.2 Battery

Most smartphones are powered by lithium-ion batteries which may be either removable or irremovable. The power is calculated in Milliamp Hours (mAh), with the usage time of the smartphone being directly proportional to the mAh value. Nowadays, smartphones possess up to 5000 mAh, while originally they had only 2000 mAh power at the start of the smartphone revolution.

5.2.3 Global Positioning System (GPS)

The GPS helps identify the exact location of any individual in the event of a threat or any suspicious activities; it is integrated into smart devices so that the owner can be found in an emergency.

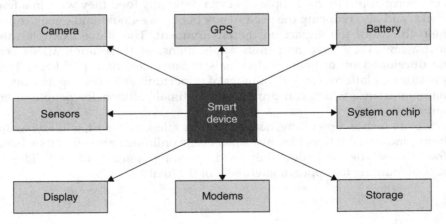

FIGURE 5.1
Smart device components.

5.2.4   Storage

In the past a 5-inch floppy disk was used to store data in the form of kilobytes. However, in the mid-1990s, these started to be replaced, and new storage systems such as external hard disks, pen drives, memory cards and many other storage devices became available. Now an individual can save Terabytes in their storage device, as well as intelligent devices being able to store a large volume of data.

5.3   Disruptive Technology

Every day technology reduces the work of humans through the innovation of solutions, as per the needs of society. A few years ago, computers were used only by a few individuals as they were very expensive. Those computers were large in size and had low performance in terms of speed, accuracy, efficiency, and other parameters, which later started to evolve. In comparison to the gadgets or the systems that are being used currently, they now possess increasingly huge storage memory, speed, accuracy and efficiency (Boccardi et al. 2004).

Disruptive technology is a process of innovation in technology that has led society to change the way it consumes and uses data by reducing the work of individuals (Danneels and Erwin 2004) and increasing the productivity in industry resulting in greater revenue for companies with lower investment costs. In real time, one web application can be a disruptive technology for the company; an application for booking a cab at the doorstep is an example of the evolution of disruptive technology. Similarly, there are many real-time situations where people have benefitted from the technology..

For example, an innovation is an electric car that replaces the need for fossil fuel, and so disrupts the current version; in that case, it may not be supported by the new owners.

5.3.1   Evolution of Disruptive Technology

Clayton Christensen sparked the discussion of disruptive technology in *The Innovator's Dilemma* in 1997. This turned out to be a buzzword in all organizations that needed to provide a product with massive productivity (Subramanian, Ramesh, and Brian 2004). The major success of disruptive technology is that every startup company focuses on promoting and innovating something new so that they can their workload as well as increase productivity. Most disruptive technology follows this principle of reduction and increase as per the needs of their customers (Subramanian, Ramesh, and Brian 2004). In simple terms, disruptive technology is not only innovating something new that was not previously in the industry, it is the process of making a change in something already in existence. That change can give benefits in terms of speed, accuracy, endurance, and so on. It disrupts the current market, while producing a new market (Nassir et al., 2015).

5.3.2 Types of Disruptive Technology

Disruptive technologies are evolving faster as there has been development in all forms of technology, such as artificial intelligence, augmented reality, 3D printing, cloud computing, the Internet of Things, space colonization, autonomous vehicles, renewable energy, and high-speed travel.

Disruptive technology can be categorized by the latest and most important emerging mechanisms.

To summarize, the major disruptive technologies include:

1. Cloud computing
2. Internet of Things
3. Blockchain
4. Virtual/augmented reality
5. Artificial intelligence
6. 3D printing
7. Space colonization
8. Autonomous vehicles
9. Renewable energy
10. High-speed travel.

5.3.2.1 *Cloud Computing*

This is one of the disruptive technologies that has disrupted the traditional database, which used to store the data in remote locations, whereas the cloud stores the data itself, where users are able to access the data from any location. Cloud computing is the process of storing data on any server which is connected to the Internet 24/7 (Velte et al. 2009).

It provides the services such as infrastructure, including the server, printer, database, and other hardware components, a platform such as an operating system which is not available for free, software such as a few versions which are not affordable by the user, so that he/she can rent the application for as long as needed.

In Figure 5.2, it can be seen that the disruptions for storing data occur in many forms, such as file management system, database management system, cloud computing, fog computing and edge computing.

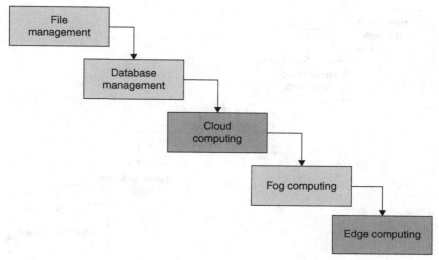

FIGURE 5.2
Disruption in storing the data.

5.3.2.2 *Internet of Things*

The Internet of Things (IoT) is the innovation carried out by a wireless sensor network and cloud computing, as the sensors are used to capture environmental changes such as temperature, gas, humidity, and so on, while the cloud is integrated with the sensors by a GSM network to send the data which can then be sent to the user as a notification (Minhaj Ahmad, and Khaled Salah 2018).

Figure 5.3 illustrates the evolution in transferring data which started with the interaction of humans only for any exchange of information. The Internet came, where people used the world wide web (WWW) to discover any information they required, as it could be retrieved through the Internet, which was the beginning of the evolution of disruptive technology in terms of data sharing. It then was transferred as web services like e-commerce. Social media then emerged as solid digital media, followed by the innovation of sensors and the Internet, leading to the Internet of Things.

5.3.2.3 *Blockchain*

Blockchain results in a decentralized system not owned by a single individual. It contains unchangeable data records, where there is no disruption in the involvement of central servers, and the communication is "peer to peer" (Li et al. 2020). Any individuals can access the database, and it is transparent. Blockchain can be implemented in three forms: private, public and

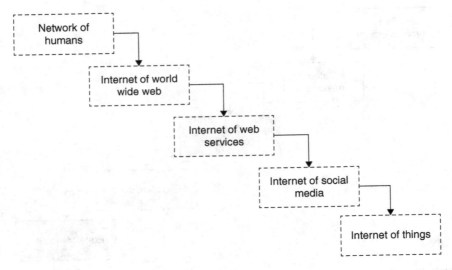

FIGURE 5.3
Disruption in transferring the data.

consortium area. Blockchain can be used to increase the security of the IoT by identity and an access management system (Singh et al. 2020)

Here, the information is distributed but not copied. It was developed for digital currency initially, but has now found other potential uses (Zhou et al. 2020).

5.3.2.3.1 *Advantages*

- No transaction cost
- No duplicate data
- No centralized server
- Faster transactions
- Immutable records
- Encrypted data
- Transparency
- Efficiency
- Speed
- Reduced cost.

The above are just some of its advantages.

TABLE 5.1

Blockchain Components with Description

S. no	Component Name	Description
1.	Consensus	This gives the proof of work and validates the event in the network.
2.	Ledger	This gives the transaction details in the network.
3.	Cryptography	This ensures that all the data are encrypted and decrypted before sending and receiving.
4.	Smart contract	This authenticates the user of the network.

5.3.2.3.2 Components of Blockchain

There are four main components associated with blockchain as described in Table 5.1.

5.3.2.4 Virtual/Augmented Reality

5.3.2.4.1 Augmented Reality

Digital images are superimposed into a real-world environment, providing a view of an illusion or virtual reality (Williams et al. 2019). AR combines the natural world with the virtual world and the interaction between the two different worlds for enhancing communication. Nowadays, even smartphones have begun to possess the property of augmented reality. Many researchers have been working to make the virtual environment livelier so that no difference can be seen between the real and virtual surroundings (Williams et al. 2019; Verhey et al. 2020).

The applications of augmented reality include:

- Healthcare
- Industry
- Visualization
- Robotics navigation
- Entertainment
- Military aircraft
- Design and modeling
- Logistics
- Tourism and travel.

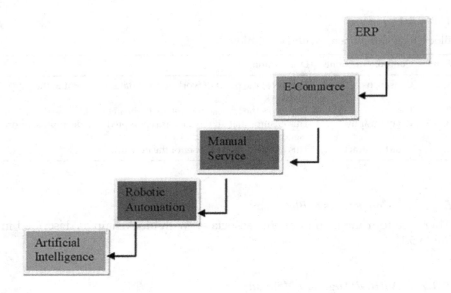

FIGURE 5.4
AI evolution.

5.3.2.5 *Artificial Intelligence (AI)*

AI is the process of simulating the thinking of humans in machines, where the machine is programmed to think like a human when a certain situation occurs to the device (Jackson and Philip 2019). The primary objective of AI is to attain the best decision for any critical situation that is happening to the machines (Szolovits and Peter 2019).

Its three major objectives include:

1. Learning
2. Reasoning
3. Perception.

Figure 5.4 illustrates the changes that have occurred in the manual and automation areas by humans and robots.

5.3.2.6 *3D Printing*

This is used in the manufacture of physical objects where the materials are deposited in digital model layers. The 3D printer needs hardware, software and materials for printing. It has started to replace traditional manufacturing methods as it takes less time to produce and most significantly it has less of an impact on the environment (Chen et al. 2019).

The application starts with a prototype of any material including high-end products such as aircraft parts, environment-friendly buildings, medical plants, and organs produced artificially by human cells.

The methods for printing 3D objects include:

- Fused filament fabrication (FFF)
- Stereolithography (SLA).

5.3.2.6.1 *Advantages of 3D Printing*

- Faster build
- Less waste generation
- Less cost
- Reduced errors
- Demand-based production
- Quality
- Unlimited design
- Risk reduction.

5.3.2.7 Autonomous Vehicles

These vehicles have the potential to sense the environment, and driving can be done without the help of humans; it can travel to the same places as a driver-based car, while this driverless car will never need any support from humans as once the data are provided, it will start learning by itself. It can reach the desired places that the user wishes without them having to take control; if the user needs to go to the office, he/she can do so by a verbal instruction (Faisal et al. 2019).

It has been implemented using various sensors such as radar sensors, ultrasonic sensors and Lidar (light detection and ranging) along with GPS and video cameras (Faisal et al. 2019).

5.3.2.7.1 *Benefits of Autonomous Vehicles*

- They can decrease the number of vehicles in the road, leading to less traffic congestion, as it will be aware of the fastest route automatically by GPS.
- It can reduce transportation costs as the vehicle will be used only to reach the required place and finds the best route to reach the destination.

5.3.2.8 Renewable Energy

Energy obtained from any natural means or repeated processes is called clean energy (Infield, David, and Leon Freris 2020). Renewable energy has been classified in Figure 5.5.

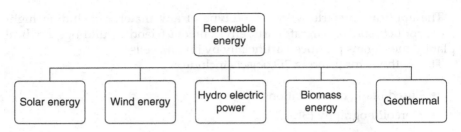

FIGURE 5.5
Classification of renewable energy.

5.3.2.8.1 *Benefits of Renewable Energy*

- It produces less gas emissions than other energy systems as it works on the principle of being replenished by nature, which can reduce the problems associated with global warming.
- It helps in improving the health of humans when they use renewable energy as it reduces diseases transmitted through air and water.
- The process is never-ending as the cycle keeps repeating itself with available energy resources to produce new energy.

5.4 Cryptography Algorithms for Securing IoT Devices through Blockchain

5.4.1 Cryptography

This is the process of securing information from intruders who are not authorized to use it; in simple terms, the information is encoded and sent to the user with the key, which is used to decode the data to allow them to be read and accessed. The key is difficult for an intruder or attacker to crack as it is based on an algorithm (Pirandola et al. 2019).

This word is derived from Greek kryptos; and it started to be used as early as 2000 BCE in Egypt. It can be divided and described in the following way as:

Crypt = Hidden and Graphy = Writing

The above meaning illustrates that code is written in a hidden way so that only privileged users can access the information.

5.4.1.1 Benefits of Cryptography

There are many advantages associated with encrypting data before transmission, with some of the major benefits including the following (Pirandola et al. 2019):

- Application of different heterogeneous devices is possible by using a cryptography algorithm.
- It helps employees to work in remote locations if needed without any security issues.
- It promotes the privacy of data for the customer, to achieve maximum safeguarding of data.
- It gives trust to the customers of companies by using an encryption algorithm for data transmission, which leads to increased revenue. The process of cryptography has been described in Figure 5.6. Cryptography can be classified according to the encryption keys as shown in Figure 5.7.

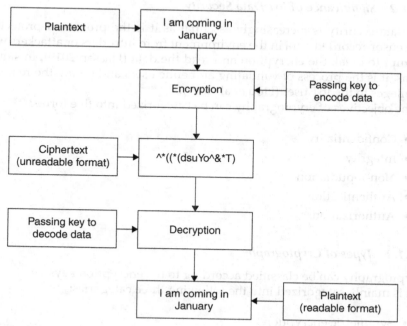

FIGURE 5.6
Cryptography process.

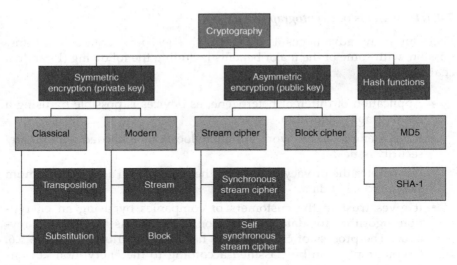

FIGURE 5.7
Cryptography classification.

5.4.1.2 Significance of IoT Data Security

IoT data security is increasingly essential as it is the process of protecting the sensor-recorded data in the environment from intruders or attackers who attempt to break the encryption and read the data (Hassan 2019). In simple terms, it is the process of validating authentic users and giving the required privileges to the IoT user (Hou et al. 2019).

The objectives of cryptography can be categorized into five forms:

- Confidentiality
- Integrity
- Non-repudiation
- Authentication
- Authorization.

5.4.1.3 Types of Cryptography

Cryptography can be classified according to the encryption keys.
It is mainly categorized into the following three categories:

- Symmetric encryption
- Asymmetric encryption
- Hash functions.

5.4.1.4 Symmetric Encryption

In this method, a single key is used for both encryption and decryption by the sender as well as the receiver, this single key is called a private or secret key (Li et al. 2019).

- Examples: AES (Advanced Encryption Standard)
- Data Encryption System (DES), Triple DES, RC2, RC4, RC5, IDEA, Blowfish, Stream cipher, Block cipher.

5.4.1.5 Asymmetric Encryption

In this type of encryption there are two keys, public access which is used for encryption, and the private key which is used for decryption. The advantage of this encryption method is that the public and private keys are different. Therefore if an intruder compromises one key, it is not possible for them to breach the message.

Examples: Diffie Hellman key exchange algorithm, RSA algorithm.

5.4.1.6 Hash Functions

These are the mathematical notations whereby one number is changed into another value with a smaller value. The significant advantage of this function is that the input can be of any length, but the output always will be of a fixed length. It is more essential in applications which need to provide maximum security. The most efficient hash functions for the IoT environment are SHA-1 and MD5. The most efficient hash functions for the IoT environment are SHA-1 and MD5, as shown in Figure 5.8.

5.4.1.7 Blockchain-Integrated IoT System

Blockchain can be used to enhance IoT security as it is a decentralized environment, where it cannot be tracked by an intruder for the location of data (Patel et al. 2020). It can bridge the gap of security, privacy and scalability issues in the IoT environment. The decentralized architecture makes the data be stored in servers in multiple locations, and so a single point of failure will not affect the recorded data, unlike with a cloud-based IoT system, where data is held in a single place, leading to lost data in the case of a crash in the cloud server (Mistry et al. 2020).

5.4.1.8 Components of Blockchain

Blockchain consists of the major components described in Table 5.2.

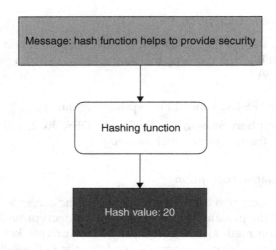

FIGURE 5.8
Hashing function.

TABLE 5.2

Components of Blockchain

S. no	Components	Description
1.	Network of nodes	Proof of work verifies the transaction authenticity in the network.
2.	Distributed database system	In the database, each block consists of a timestamp and transaction that provides the required additional information.
3.	Ledger	This is available to all users and is updated throughout the transaction whenever the user updates the data.
4.	Cryptography	All data must be encrypted ,which ensure the safeguarding of data security.

5.4.1.9   Types of Blockchain

Blockchain can be classified in two major ways, as described in Figure 5.9.

5.4.1.9.1   Private Blockchain

In this environment, trusted and well-known users are used to carry out the read and write operations.

5.4.1.9.2   Public Blockchain

In this environment anybody can have access to read or write the data. Bitcoins are the best example of those using the public blockchain.

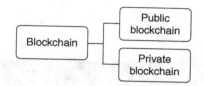

FIGURE 5.9
Types of blockchain.

5.4.1.10 Blockchain Integration in the IoT

The primary reason for incorporating the IoT with blockchain is to enhance the privacy and security of the IoT environment, as intruders can compromise the IoT cloud servers at any time. Many companies have started to integrate the IoT with blockchain to achieve maximum production and supply chains (Wazid et al. 2020).

It gives transparency when products are in logistics, which increases the customer's trust of the product. Some companies have started to use decentralized server models for their working operations (Tseng et al. 2020).

The identity and access management system can enhance IoT security by using blockchain; these systems store data about digital rights, identity and user credentials. It may vigorously defend against attacks such as man in the middle attacks, application-layer attacks and IP spoofing.

5.4.1.11 Cloud Models

In the IoT cloud, devices are connected and data are stored on servers; even the sensor and cloud are close to each other. Still, it must be associated with the Internet to transfer the IoT data.

The first concern will be the cost factor as the data need cloud and Internet connection, irrespective of the distance between the server and the IoT environment. The second factor will be security, as the information is stored in the cloud, which is open to intruders or hackers, as the IoT environment is open to frequent attacks such as DDOS, IP spoofing and so on. The third factor will be the downtime of the cloud if it has been affected by the intruder attacks, where the IoT user will not be able to access the actual data or the data can be altered.

5.4.1.12 Advantages of Blockchain in the IoT

The combination of the IoT with blockchain has improved quality of life for many people and in many ways; a few major benefits are described in the following, as shown in Figure 5.10:

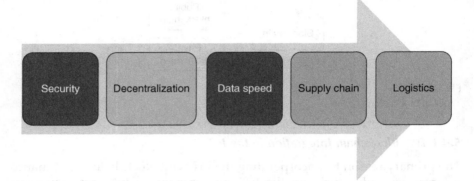

FIGURE 5.10
Advantages of blockchain in the IoT.

1. The speed of data transfer can be more efficient by integrating blockchain with the IoT environment.
2. As blockchain is all about decentralization, it can reduce the operational cost of the IoT as it is not using the centralized server only.
3. One of the major concerns for the IoT environment is security, which can be enhanced by using blockchain as it trusts only legitimate users.
4. As the speed of transactions increases and there is a reduction in cost, it leads to another great advantage: supply chain efficiency.
5. Industries such as medicine and others which needs logistics can use IoT blockchain to support the transfer of goods.

5.4.2 Cryptographic Algorithm through Blockchain

5.4.2.1 *IoT Security Attacks*

An attack is an event that disturbs the normal flow of the execution of the IoT environment, where the attack can be made by an intruder, attacker, or hacker who should not be able to access the information but through direct or indirect attacks has gained access to the IoT environment (Jain, Anshul, and Tanya Singh 2020).

The significant challenges included recorded data stored in the centralized server/cloud where the user may access data whenever needed. However, the issue is that the cloud is constantly open to the Internet, which makes it easy for intruders to make "N" number of attacks, such as brute force, IP spoofing, a man in the middle attack or compromised attack to obtain data from the server (Alam et al. 2020).

5.5 Augmented Reality in Transactions with Blockchain Protection

5.5.1 Augmented Reality

This is the process in which a natural environment is created that is not real but similar to real-world experience. It is achieved using computer-generated sensor input such as visual, audio and sensor models. The program must be used to create a virtual environment where the user can have real-time interaction with any individual who is not available at the location but still able to make an environment which is very real (Palmarin et al. 2018).

5.5.2 Components of Augmented Reality Architecture

The augmented reality components and working are displayed in Figure 5.11.

- Hardware requirements
- Virtual location
- Real location.

5.5.2.1 Virtual Location

This is a replication of the natural environment using a hardware environment. The real-time environment is presented digitally, such as 3D animation,

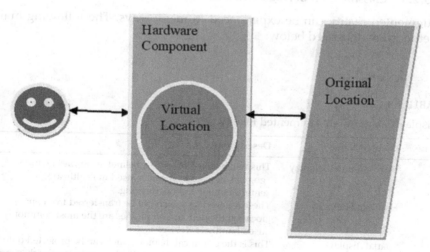

FIGURE 5.11
Augmented reality architecture.

2D images, websites and vibrations. The primary feature of augmented reality is that virtual content can be changed dynamically.

5.5.2.2   Real Location

This consists of the geographic location, physical objects and environment used to make it more lifelike to the augmented reality users; when viewing the augmented reality, users will be able to look at the location's natural environment.

5.5.2.3   Hardware Requirements

This include components such as:

- Processor
- Display
- Sensors
- Input devices
- Camera.

5.5.2.4   Display

This consist of three major components as described in Table 5.3.

5.5.2.5   Classification of Augmented Reality Tools

Augmented reality can be experienced in many ways. The following main methods are discussed below:

TABLE 5.3

Display Categories in Augmented Reality

S. no	Display Name	Description
1	Head-mounted display	This will be fixed on or to a helmet, examples include goggles or glasses. It can be used in healthcare, entertainment and engineering.
2	Handheld device	These are devices which can be transferred from one location to another. Cell phones are the most commonly used handheld device.
3	Spatial display	This is the graphical display which can be projected onto any fixed surface, and can display time series such as grid, scalar, polygon.

1. Augmented reality 3D viewers
2. Augmented reality browsers
3. Augmented reality gaming.

5.5.2.6 Ways to Create Augmented Reality Applications

There are three major possible ways to create augmented reality applications, as also shown in Figure 5.12:

- Marker based
- Markerless based
- Location based.

5.5.2.7 Marker Based

These are based on image identification, which uses black and white markers to display AR content. The augmented component can be used whenever the camera is placed around the marker location.

For example:

In the education system, a concept can be taught in multiple ways such as board teaching, webinar, online tutorials, flipped class and so on. AR can make the system seem more alive by inserting animations into the pages of a book, and so, whenever the student points the camera at the text, the animation lecture will start automatically, making understanding the subject matter much easier for the students.

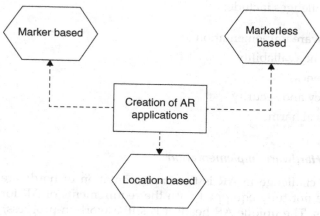

FIGURE 5.12
Creation of AR applications.

5.5.2.8   Markerless Based

This helps the user to choose different options in the environment, where the location is not mandatory. The user can decide to fix a virtual object in "N" possible ways and get the best choice in a particular category.

For example:

In a university, when a new auditorium is built for the students, it is not possible to predict the exact number of chairs for the seminar hall; at this moment, the concept of the markerless-based method can give a visualization of the right and appropriate collections to the environment.

5.5.2.9   Location Based

This works on location by using an accelerometer, digital compass and GPS. Pokemon GO is a very famous AR game that works based on location. Additionally, it can help us to locate cars in an extensive parking system.

For example:

If a user wants to travel to a new place, which he/she knows nothing about, then this AR will help by showing the navigation virtually with street name, location and complete address of the location in an interactive way.

5.5.2.10   Challenges in Augmented Reality

Although there are many AR applications associated with education, manufacturing, healthcare, transportation (such as airport) and entertainment (such as movies), there remain many challenges to the implementation of AR in the real world (Al-Shuwaili, Ali, and Osvaldo Simeone 2017), as shown in Figure 5.13.

These challenges include:

- Hardware implementation
- Content availability
- Awareness
- Privacy and security
- Physical harm.

5.5.2.11   Hardware Implementation

The major challenge in AR is the implementation of hardware, as mobile devices are not fully equipped with the requirements of AR for interactive experiences. The unique AR headset is still a work-in-progress, as the consumer needs the headsets to experience the virtual environment more interactively (Al-Shuwaili, Ali, and Osvaldo Simeone 2017).

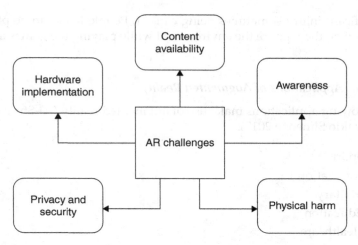

FIGURE 5.13
Augmented reality challenges.

5.5.2.12 Content Availability

The main requirement of augmented reality is the content, as it will make the environment attractive. Companies face challenges in the generation of quality content.

5.5.2.13 Awareness about the Technology

As people showed interest in Pokémon and Ingress, they reached a significantly too large audience. Still, knowledge about AR has not reached all audiences, as not all AR-based games have gained sufficient recognition and have used inefficient applications. Therefore, marketing remains one of the most significant challenges in AR.

5.5.2.14 Privacy and Security

The challenge in augmented reality is that there are no standard measures (right or wrong intentions) to assess it, which leads the user to have security problems. As the knowledge about AR is still insufficient, it can lead to both issues of privacy and security. An intruder or hacker can breach the system by slightly altering the security mechanism (Al-Shuwaili, Ali, and Osvaldo Simeone 2017).

5.5.2.15 Physical Harm

The most worrying challenging about AR is the lack of attention to the environment, which can lead to accidents in few cases, with minor as well as significant injury sometimes being caused. People lives can be placed in danger when they ignore the environment while playing the games in public places.

5.5.2.16   Applications of Augmented Reality

The following applications make use of augmented reality (Al-Shuwaili, Ali, and Osvaldo Simeone 2017):

1. Sports
2. Navigation
3. Military
4. Education
5. Healthcare
6. Advertising
7. Maintenance
8. Tourism.

References

1. Boccardi, Federico, Robert W. Heath, Angel Lozano, Thomas L. Marzetta, and Petar Popovski (2014). Five disruptive technology directions for 5G. *IEEE Communications Magazine*, 52(2), 74–80.
2. Danneels, Erwin (2004). Disruptive technology reconsidered: A critique and research agenda. *Journal of Product Innovation Management*, 21(4), 246–258.
3. Subramanian, Ramesh, and Brian D. Goodman (Eds.) (2005). *Peer-to-Peer Computing: The Evolution of a Disruptive Technology*. IGI Global, USA.
4. Nassiri, Nima, Shyam Natarajan, Daniel J. Margolis, and Leonard S. Marks (2015). Targeted prostate biopsy: Lessons learned midst the evolution of a disruptive technology. *Urology*, 86(3), 432–438.
5. Velte, Toby, Anthony Velte, and Robert Elsenpeter (2009). *Cloud Computing, a Practical Approach*. McGraw-Hill, Inc., USA
6. Khan, Minhaj Ahmad, and Khaled Salah (2018). IoT security: Review, blockchain solutions, and open challenges. *Future Generation Computer Systems*, 82, 395–411.
7. Singh, Sushil Kumar, Shailendra Rathore, and Jong Hyuk Park (2020). Blockiotintelligence: A blockchain-enabled intelligent IoT architecture with artificial intelligence. *Future Generation Computer Systems*, 110, 721–743.
8. Li, Xiaoqi, Peng Jiang, Ting Chen, Xiapu Luo, and Qiaoyan Wen (2020). A survey on the security of blockchain systems. *Future Generation Computer Systems*, 107, 841–853.

9. Zhou, Qiheng, Huawei Huang, Zibin Zheng, and Jing Bian (2020). Solutions to scalability of blockchain: A survey. *IEEE Access*, *8*, 16440–16455.
10. Williams, Tom, Daniel Szafir, Tathagata Chakraborti, and Elizabeth Phillips (2019). Virtual, augmented, and mixed reality for human-robot interaction (vam-hri). In *2019 14th ACM/IEEE International Conference on Human-Robot Interaction (HRI)*, pp. 671–672. IEEE.
11. Verhey, Jens T., Jack M. Haglin, Erik M. Verhey, and David E. Hartigan (2020). Virtual, augmented, and mixed reality applications in orthopedic surgery. *The International Journal of Medical Robotics and Computer Assisted Surgery*, *16*(2), e2067.
12. Szolovits, Peter (Ed.) (2019). *Artificial Intelligence in Medicine*. Routledge, New York.
13. Jackson, Philip C. (2019) *Introduction to Artificial Intelligence*. Courier Dover Publications, USA.
14. Chen, Zhangwei, Ziyong Li, Junjie Li, Chengbo Liu, Changshi Lao, Yuelong Fu, Changyong Liu, Yang Li, Pei Wang, and Yi He (2019). 3D printing of ceramics: A review. *Journal of the European Ceramic Society*, *39*(4), 661–687.
15. Campa, Riccardo, Konrad Szocik, and Martin Braddock (2019). Why space colonization will be fully automated. *Technological Forecasting and Social Change*, *143*, 162–171.
16. Faisal, Asif, Md Kamruzzaman, Tan Yigitcanlar, and Graham Currie (2019). Understanding autonomous vehicles. *Journal of Transport and Land Use*, *12*(1), 45–72.
17. Infield, David, and Leon Freris (2020). *Renewable Energy in Power Systems*. John Wiley & Sons, USA.
18. Pirandola, Stefano, Ulrik L. Andersen, Leonardo Banchi, Mario Berta, Darius Bunandar, Roger Colbeck, Dirk Englund, et al (2019). Advances in quantum cryptography. *arXiv* preprint, arXiv:1906.01645.
19. Hou, Jianwei, Leilei Qu, and Wenchang Shi (2019). A survey on internet of things security from data perspectives. *Computer Networks*, *148*, 295–306.
20. Hassan, W.H. (2019). Current research on Internet of Things (IoT) security: A survey. *Computer Networks*, *148*, 283–294.
21. Li, Jin, Yanyu Huang, Yu Wei, Siyi Lv, Zheli Liu, Changyu Dong, and Wenjing Lou (2019). Searchable symmetric encryption with forward search privacy. *IEEE Transactions on Dependable and Secure Computing* 18(1), 460–474.
22. Mistry, Ishan, Sudeep Tanwar, Sudhanshu Tyagi, and Neeraj Kumar (2020). Blockchain for 5G-enabled IoT for industrial automation: A systematic review, solutions, and challenges. *Mechanical Systems and Signal Processing*, *135*, 106382.
23. Patel, Vishwani, Fenil Khatiwala, Kaushal Shah, and Yashi Choksi (2020). A review on blockchain technology: Components, issues and challenges. In *ICDSMLA 2019*, pp. 1257–1262. Springer, Singapore.
24. Wazid, Mohammad, Ashok Kumar Das, Sachin Shetty, and Minho Jo (2020). A tutorial and future research for building a blockchain-based secure communication scheme for internet of intelligent things. *IEEE Access*, *8*, 88700–88716.
25. Tseng, Lewis, Liwen Wong, Safa Otoum, Moayad Aloqaily, and Jalel Ben Othman (2020). Blockchain for managing heterogeneous internet of things: A perspective architecture. *IEEE Network*, *34*(1), 16–23.

26. Jain, Anshul, and Tanya Singh (2020). Security challenges and solutions of IoT ecosystem. In *Information and Communication Technology for Sustainable Development*, pp. 259–270. Springer, Singapore.

27. Alam, Shadab, Shams Tabrez Siddiqui, Ausaf Ahmad, Riaz Ahmad, and Mohammed Shuaib (2020). Internet of Things (IoT) enabling technologies, requirements, and security challenges. In *Advances in Data and Information Sciences*, pp. 119–126. Springer, Singapore.

28. Palmarini, Riccardo, John Ahmet Erkoyuncu, Rajkumar Roy, and Hosein Torabmostaedi (2018). A systematic review of augmented reality applications in maintenance. *Robotics and Computer-Integrated Manufacturing, 49*, 215–228.

29. Al-Shuwaili, Ali, and Osvaldo Simeone (2017). Energy-efficient resource allocation for mobile edge computing-based augmented reality applications. *IEEE Wireless Communications Letters, 6*(3), 398–401.

6

Future Enhancements and Application of the IoT, AI and Blockchain

6.1 Implementing Blockchain, AI and IoT in Smart Cities

6.1.1 Smart City

The smart city is defined as an urban area where a group of different sensors are used to record data from the area. The recorded data are used to obtain insights about the resources, management of assets, and efficient services. The data are received from people through sensors. The smart city is a combination of information and communication technology (ICT) and sensors that send data to the IoT cloud, optimizing the city's operations and making people's lives easier at an affordable cost [1].

6.1.2 Objectives of a Smart City

The primary objective of a smart city is to ease people's lives by integrating healthcare, transportation, education, and traffic in a single environment [2], including:

- Water
- E-governance
- CO_2 emissions
- Energy
- Security
- Social innovation
- Transportation.

6.1.3 Architecture of a Smart City

Smart city architecture includes three components: artificial intelligence, blockchain and IoT devices [3]. These components have a unique ability to

DOI: 10.1201/9781003046462-7

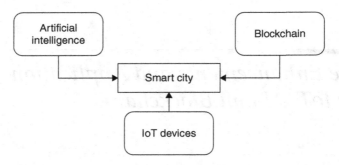

FIGURE 6.1
Integration of the IoT, AI and blockchain in a smart city.

perform a specific operation, such as AI, to carry out the work of human beings. In contrast, IoT devices record and store data, as shown in Figure 6.1.

6.1.4 Challenges in a Smart City

The smart city gives many benefits to the people, however certain challenges need to be addressed when implementing a smart city. The following are some of the identified challenges associated with implanting a smart city which need to be discussed at the construction phase [4]:

- Building infrastructure
- Privacy concerns
- Heterogeneous devices
- Efficiency
- Scalability
- Awareness to citizens
- Application development
- Cost and affordability.

6.1.5 Smart City Components

The major components of a smart city are listed in Figure 6.2.

6.1.6 Blockchain Integration with Smart Cities

6.1.6.1 Smart Health

This is a healthcare-based system where users are embedded with wearable devices, in-home sensors and mobile applications with the Internet. This

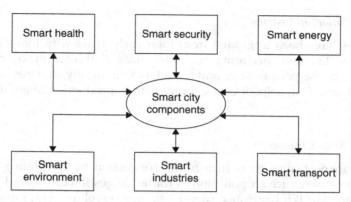

FIGURE 6.2
Smart city components.

methodology helps track people's health online and alerts if any abnormalities should occur to the user [5].

6.1.6.2   Smart Security

Sensors are embedded in doors and walls inside the home, alerting the user if any threat enters the house by sending notifications to the user; CCTV footage enhances the security and is easily customizable. Many companies have started to provide various smart security mechanisms that reassure people about the safety of their belongings when they are away from home [5].

6.1.6.3   Smart Energy

In smart energy, devices are used for producing energy; it uses renewable energy sources with affordable cost and keeps the environment clean. Solar energy and natural gas are two examples of smart energy [5].

6.1.6.4   Smart Environment

The environment which is connected with sensors, the Internet and computers can be described as a smart environment.
   Technologies of a smart environment include

1.   Human speech recognition
2.   Wireless communication between devices
3.   Operating system in computers
4.   Networking of devices
5.   Software architecture frameworks.

6.1.6.5 Smart Industries

Industries have been upgraded from their early years with many features. According to their performance, enterprises that can make decisions according to the performance and are adaptable for any changes as per the requirements. This helps increase an industry's production at an affordable cost [6].

6.1.6.6 Smart Transport

Smart transport aims to reduce traffic congestion by navigating vehicles and helping to reduce air pollution as traffic congestion can solved by using smart transport [7]. Users also spend less time traveling, with minimal cost and lower energy consumption for vehicles [5].

6.1.6.7 Blockchain Transaction Flow

Figure 6.3 explains the transaction flow in blockchain, where it starts with the user's request to complete a transaction [8].

6.1.6.8 Characteristics of Blockchain in Smart City

The primary reason that so much focus has been on blockchain is the features that are associated with it [9], which include:

- Anonymity
- Auditability
- Decentralization
- Distributed ledger
- Persistency
- Privacy.

6.1.6.8.1 Anonymity

Every user interacts with the blockchain with a generated address, where the user address is not revealed to anyone, making the user anonymous to any intruders [10].

6.1.6.8.2 Auditability

In blockchain, any transaction will be authenticated and authorized before it gets added to the blockchain. Here the transmission is verified [10].

6.1.6.8.3 Decentralization

There is a centralized system in the traditional method, which performs the transaction. The challenging factor for this is that an intruder attack on the

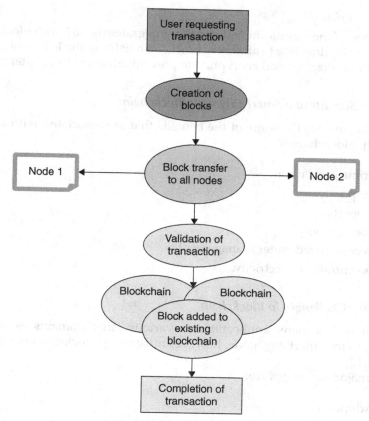

FIGURE 6.3
Blockchain transaction flow.

central server can lead to a loss of the entire network. Currently, using a decentralized system, no intruders are able to gain access to the system [10].

6.1.6.8.4 *Distributed Ledger*

This public ledger contains all users who enter the system and provides details about the transaction of all users. All blockchain users manage this ledger. This computation is shared among the computers, making it an efficient ledger.

6.1.6.8.5 *Persistency*

In the blockchain, a transaction which is occurring can be authenticated quickly, and the proxy transaction will not be taken into account by users. It is challenging to delete the transaction once it has taken place in the system, but an invalid transaction can be detected immediately.

6.1.6.8.6   Privacy

This is one of the significant features that integrates the IoT with blockchain; as the IoT is vulnerable to attackers, blockchain helps in the IoT environment with decentralization and encryption to prevent intruders from entering [11].

6.1.6.9   Benefits of a Smart City with Blockchain

The following are the some of the benefits that are associated with a smart city with blockchain:

- Crime prevention
- Corporate
- Property
- Construction
- Decentralized water management
- Decentralized electricity.

6.1.6.10   Challenges in Blockchain

Blockchain has many applications in various other domains as it is not limited to the smart city alone, however integrating blockchain has difficulties [11,12].

The major challenges are:

- Adoption
- Technology barriers
- Security risks
- Legal and regulatory issue
- Interoperability risk
- Energy consumption.

6.1.6.11   Challenges of Secured IoT

There are many researches carried out in the IoT every day on enhancing its security, however the biggest challenges that lead to security issues are due to the IoT environment [13,14], these include:

- ✓ Centralized architecture
- ✓ IoT environment
- ✓ Scalability
- ✓ Storage space

✓ Processing time
✓ Devices reliability.

6.1.6.12 *Centralized Architecture*

As the data in the IoT are stored in a centralized cloud, this makes it easier for hackers to intrude into the system and attack the cloud server, which leads to loss of the confidentiality, availability and integrity of the data. This can be recovered by using the blockchain concept, as there is no centralized system in the transmission of data [15].

6.1.6.13 *IoT Environment*

The IoT environment is composed of sensors, actuators, embedded devices and servers. It collects data from heterogeneous devices, however, as there is no unique mechanism for all heterogeneous devices, the major challenging factor is the connection among different types of devices, making it difficult to detect any failure of a single device from a large number of devices.

6.1.6.14 *Scalability*

The primary requirement of an IoT device is to possess scalability as it is a collection of heterogeneous devices connected to different individuals, therefore it is difficult to obtain the property of scalability [16], and it involves the process of handling a large amount of data in a particular network or system. It reduces the risks in the IoT and simplifies recording of the environment [17].

6.1.6.15 *Storage Space*

In the IoT data are recorded continuously and stored in the cloud. These data need a huge volume for storage. These data may be not essential after a specific duration of time. Therefore the cloud service provider manages the server space for the future, where the redundant data may be removed with the knowledge of the user.

6.1.6.16 *Processing Time*

The main advantage of the IoT is the distance between the user and the IoT environment where the user will be able to access the data irrespective of his/her location; if the space is nominal, then the access time and notifications will be faster and reliable, but the issue arises when the user reaches the maximum limit, which may lead to a delay in the processing time of the IoT devices.

6.1.6.17 Devices Reliability

In the IoT ecosystem, each sensor is connected to the central server, which the cloud, as cloud computing is the process of storing data on a rental basis by the service level agreement (SLA). Even if the server's location is near the sensors, it must be connected to establish the connection.

6.1.6.18 Artificial Intelligence

Artificial intelligence involves is the method of making systems think like humans without human intervention; in simple terms, human intelligence is imparted to machines. This will reduce the work of humans and can help in large-scale production. It can work with qualitative and quantitative data [18].

It can be mainly categorized into two streams:

1. Knowledge-based systems
2. Computational intelligence.

6.1.6.19 Knowledge-Based System (KBS)

This is a knowledge base that contains all the necessary information about the domains, based on the past events, which was uploaded by users [19]. Cases, frames and rules can be described as knowledge in this category, as shown in Figure 6.4.

It carries out a reasoning mechanism, which usually would be done by humans. Heuristic methods are used in a knowledge-based system to solve associated problems. If–then rules are used in this category instead of mathematical notation.

6.1.7 Computational Intelligence (CI)

The following are the methods of computational intelligence that artificial intelligence uses [20]:

- Fuzzy system
- Generic algorithm
- Neural network.

6.1.8 Fuzzy System

In certain situations, it is impossible to predict whether something will happen or not as per the requirements. To solve this issue [21], fuzzy logic can indicate whether it is partially true or false. It possesses intermediate values between correct and wrong, as shown in Figure 6.5.

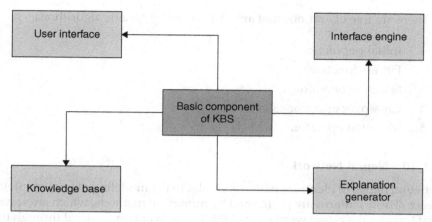

FIGURE 6.4
Basic components of a knowledge-based system.

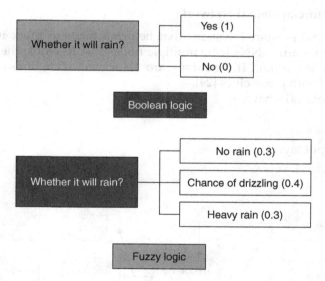

FIGURE 6.5
Fuzzy logic vs Boolean logic.

It contrasts with Boolean logic, in which there are two conditions only, either true or false. The above example compares Boolean logic and fuzzy logic.

6.1.9 Genetic Algorithm

This evolved from natural evolution as inspired by Charles Darwin. It is an adaptive heuristic approach that produces an optimal solution to any complex problem [22].

There are five operations that are carried out by genetic algorithms:

1. Initial population
2. Fitness function
3. Selection operator
4. Crossover operator
5. Mutation operator.

6.1.10   Neural Network

A neural network identifies patterns similar to the modeling of human intelligence. These patterns are performed by numerical methods, which are scalar, that transfer the actual word entity [23]. The data are understood through the intervention of the machine, as shown in Figure 6.6.

6.1.11   Artificial Neural Networks

These are brain-inspired systems that help machines to think in the way that humans learn. ANNs have multiple nodes that resemble the biological neurons of the brain. The neurons are associated with links, which are interrelated with themselves [24].

Neural networks have:

1. Input layers
2. Output layers
3. Hidden layers.

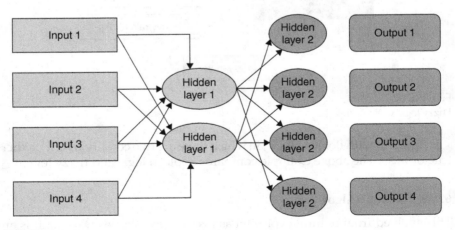

FIGURE 6.6
Neural network.

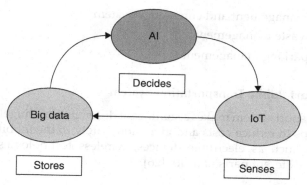

FIGURE 6.7
Integration of AI, the IoT and big data.

6.1.12   AI and the IoT in a Smart City

The IoT senses the data from sensors, while AI is used to instruct the IoT to record the data from the environment as the data are stored in big data. These data will then be passed back to the AI for extracting the information and making decisions based on past events that help in solving future similar problems. Figure 6.7 shows an interpretation of the data.

6.1.13   Big Data in the IoT

The extensive collection of structured, unstructured, semistructured data can be used to make decisions from large data sets. Here the data are recorded continuously from the smart city environment. This helps in taking any decisions based on the available data and increases the productivity from a business perspective.

6.1.14   Security using AI

The combination of AI and the IoT in a smart city helps in various ways [25], including:

- Weapon noise detection
- Surveillance and analytics
- Drones.

6.1.15   Application of AI in Smart Cities

- Smart public transportation system
- Intelligent traffic management and control system

- Safety management and emergency system
- Smart waste management
- Smart parking management.

6.1.16 Smart Public Transportation System

A smart transport system makes a significant difference in a hugely populated city and helps to reduce costs and give more safety to the inhbitants; it uses components such as electronic devices, wireless technologies and cloud between the different parts of a city [26].

6.1.17 Benefits

- Pollution can be reduced, which helps to reduce global warming.
- People have greater safety and security, compared to traditional methods of transport.

6.1.18 Intelligent Traffic Management and Control System

This is used to reduce the traffic in cities through an efficient traffic mechanism; it uses GPS, which helps to find the locations of vehicles and thus makes it easy for routing vehicles according to the available routes.

6.1.19 Safety Management and Emergency System

This is used to protect people from any unpredicted accidents, which may happen for many reasons. An emergency system will alert a nearby hospital, and take immediate action that can save people's lives.

6.1.20 Smart Waste Management

The IoT has the potential to reduce the cost of waste and its operational expenses by using AI [27].

Waste can be generally classified into five types, namely:

1. Organic waste
2. Recyclable waste
3. Hazardous waste
4. Solid waste
5. Liquid waste.

6.1.21   Smart Parking Management

Smart parking is crucial to address the increase in traffic congestion and unavailability of parking spaces for vehicles. Smart parking management can overcome the above challenges at nominal cost with efficient parking of vehicles [28].

6.2   Improving Clinical Diagnosis with Smart IoT Devices Using an AI Mechanism

6.2.1   Smart IoT

Wearable devices are growing at a speed where they may be able to replace mobile phones in the future.. The IoT is molding human existence with more prominent availability and extreme usefulness through universal systems administration to the Internet. It will be increasingly close to home and prescient, and consolidate the physical and virtual worlds to make an exceedingly customized and regularly proactive associated understanding [29].

The IoT still challenges researchers in security as data gets stored in the cloud, and so it can be compromised by intruders at any point in time. Without the use of solid defense at all joints of the IoT and protection of information, the advancement of the IoT will be prevented by prosecutions and social opposition. The development of the IoT would be moderate without the correct principles for the use of the associated devices and sensors.

6.2.2   Types of Biomedical IoT Sensors for Diagnosis

Sensors are used to record data from the environment through the Internet of Things, which plays a vital role in data collection. For example, a temperature sensor can alert the user if the temperature goes beyond the average level. Similarly, many sensors are used in different applications as per the individual's requirements [30].

Biomedical sensors are used to identify specific biological, physical or chemical processes. The data can then be transferred to the place where any abnormalities are noted, and precautions can taken [31]. It is often used to monitor the status of medicines, environmental conditions, food, water and other substances, such as whether it is safe to drink or eat, or any activities associated with the entity, as shown in Figure 6.8.

The sensors are classified based on their types, such as:

1.   Blood oxygen sensors
2.   Blood glucose sensors

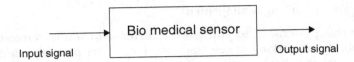

FIGURE 6.8
Biomedical sensor.

   3.   Temperature sensors

   4.   Image sensors

   5.   Pressure sensors

   6.   Inertial sensors

   7.   Motion sensors

   8.   ECG sensors.

The most commonly used sensors in biomedical instrumentation are:

   I.   Body temperature sensors

   II.   Biomedical mechanical sensors

   III.   Ultrasound imaging sensors

   IV.   Radiology detection sensors.

6.2.3   The IoT and Biomedical Instrumentation

IoT applications are used in all aspects of life such as education, transportation, agriculture, military, smart homes and so on. the most significant advantage of the IoT in healthcare is that it can be used for monitoring, warning and detecting any abnormalities in patients. It increases the betterment of humans where the role of the doctor is reduced and pressure is taken off the workforce-based system.

6.2.4   Variations of Biomedical Data

There are three different variations in biomedical data based on the storage format [32]:

   1.   Biomedical image data

   2.   Biomedical signal data

   3.   Biomedical genome data.

6.2.4.1   Biomedical Image Data

These data are used to detect patterns from images; if any abnormalities are found in the image pattern, then the specific disease, such as breast cancer or brain tumor, can be diagnosed with the help of biomedical images.

6.2.4.2 Biomedical Signal Data

This is used to realize the physiological mechanisms of certain biological systems.

6.2.4.3 Biomedical Genome Data

The genome is used to differentiate living organisms; a single human genome can hold 100 GB of data, as shown in Table 6.1.

6.2.5 Classification of Biomedical Instruments

Different types of biomedical instruments [33] are described in Figure 6.9.

6.2.5.1 Direct/Indirect

The sensing system measures directly, such as the average volume blood flow in an artery.

6.2.5.2 Invasive/Noninvasive

This includes an imaging system that can measure blood flow dynamics in an artery [34].

TABLE 6.1

Variations of Biomedical Data

S. no.	Variations of Biomedical Data	Examples
1	Biomedical image data	Magnetic resonance imaging (MRI), computed tomography (CT), functional magnetic resonance imaging (fMRI)
2	Biomedical signal data	Electrocardiography (ECG), electroencephalography (EEG), electroneurogram (ENG), electromyogram (EMG)
3	Biomedical genome data	Deoxyribonucleic acid (DNA)

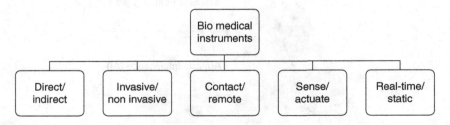

FIGURE 6.9
Classification of biomedical instruments.
Source: [34].

6.2.5.3 *Contact/Remote*

This includes one of the strain gauge sensors which are attached to a muscle fiber to track deformations due to forces in the muscle.

6.2.5.4 *Sense/Actuate*

These types detect biochemical, bioelectrical an biophysical parameters, such as an automated insulin delivery pump that is a direct, contact actuator.

6.2.5.5 *Dynamic/Static*

Static instruments measure temporal averages of physiologic parameters.

6.2.6 Integration of AI with the IoT

The IoT records a large amount of healthcare data which can be used along with AI for predicting and diagnosing diseases. AI is the process in which a computer can think and act like a human, in which testing data are given to the system. It responds to a new similar situation by providing a solution based on the data given by the user already. In simple terms, AI is a replacement of human intelligence. Figure 6.10 explains the hierarchy.

6.2.7 Healthcare Challenges in Integrating AI and the IoT

There are specific legal and ethical issues that arise with the privacy and confidentiality of IoT healthcare data. An essential aspect of healthcare is the

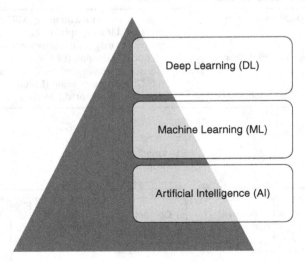

FIGURE 6.10
AI vs ML vs DL.

security of genotype data. IoT applications have many benefits; however, some challenges are associated with integrating the IoT with AI. The data recorded are primarily unstructured, and a complex algorithm is needed to generate the value from IoT data. As the data are stored in the IoT cloud, cybersecurity is required to protect sensitive data [35].

6.2.8 Medical Diagnostic Lifecycle

Figure 6.11 explains how a patient's data are recorded and then a diagnosis provided.

6.2.8.1 *Patient Data Collection*

In this phase, the patient's heart rate, BP, sugar level and all other health-related data are measured and taken into consideration. Depending upon the needs, the patient's health data can be recorded and used in diagnostics [36].

6.2.8.2 *Data Analysis*

Here the data that are collected are used to analyze the patient issues. The data help to obtain an overall summary of the patient's condition.

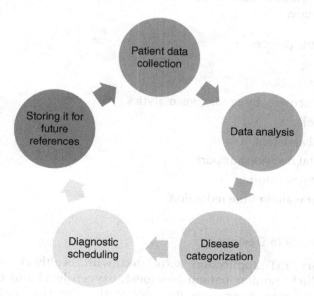

FIGURE 6.11
Medical diagnostic lifecycle.

6.2.8.3 Disease Categorization

In this phase, analyzed data are categorized and then sent to the next phase for further processing.

6.2.8.4 Diagnostic Scheduling

Once the disease has been analyzed and then categorized, it must be diagnosed as soon as possible. All prior planning is done to carry out the treatment.

6.2.8.5 Storing Data for Future Reference

Once the treatment has been carried out, irrespective of the diagnostic results, the data have to be stored in the hierarchy, where similar cases can be handled in the future.

6.2.9 AI in IoT Healthcare

AI has numerous applications in diagnosing patients based on the previous hospital records. This reduces the burden of doctors, nurses and administrators by performing tasks in less time at an affordable cost [37]. It reduce errors and enables patients to be diagnosed with maximum accuracy. It helps to detect any patient issues faster than a doctor is able to do. An AI model algorithm can diagnose breast cancer better than a pathologist. Areas covered include:

- Wearable devices
- Imaging
- Drug detection
- Risk discovery by predictive analytics
- Genomics
- Virtual assistant
- Hospital decision support
- Remote monitoring
- Patient waiting time reduction.

6.2.10 Wearable Devices

The primary IoT application associated with healthcare is wearable devices, which monitor patient heartbeat, oxygen level and other health data. Additionally, it connects the user to the cloud so that healthcare professionals are able to monitor the users for any abnormal data. This reduces the time used by both users and doctors, as visiting the hospital multiple times is not required, whereas, in the physical mode, the user has to visit the hospital each time for these health readings to be taken. There is also the possibility of infections spreading if physical presence is required for health readings [38].

6.2.11   Imaging

Medical imaging is the principal area where AI supports in helping diagnose patients. The significant advantage of medical imaging is that it can continuously monitor the patient without any break, enabling the patient to receive decisions with maximum accuracy and quickly. The disadvantage associated with AI is that it cold replace millions of jobs and lead to unemployment in the coming years.

6.2.12   Drug Detection

AI-supported drug discovery will mainly impact the pharmacy sector, but it may take time, and a lot of research needs to be carried out to make it more effective. The major challenge will be security and privacy in terms of patient data, where a genetic code is needed to produce the drug.

6.2.13   Genomics

The primary AI application is to replace human intelligence, but in clinical genomics, it can perform tasks that human intellect cannot even think of doing. A specific AI algorithm called deep learning is used to process genomic datasets. The most standard genomic methods are variant calling, genome annotation and variant classification.

6.2.14   Virtual Assistant

A virtual assistant can be defined in many ways as it varies based on the patients' need and application. It can be used in the home as well as workplaces. It is the most advanced AI technique which has yet to come to market globally at an affordable cost. Many research works are being carried out on these AI virtual assistants as the challenges are numerous.

6.2.15   Hospital Decision Support

In healthcare, making decisions using AI will give more quality data and help patients to recover mre quickly. It makes the work easier for doctors as well as others who are associated with healthcare. AI will tell precisely about the patient conditions, whether it will be possible to treat the patient or there are complications which makes it difficult to treat them.also, AI helps to accurately assess the patient's condition [39].

6.2.16 Remote Monitoring

This includes the following:

- Data acquisition system
- Data processing system
- Monitor or terminal.

6.2.17 Patient Waiting Time Reduction

AI-enabled healthcare helps to automate the monitoring and diagnosis of patients based upon the availability of resources and the number of patients that need to be analyzed. This helps match patients to available doctors, reducing time spent at the hospital.

6.3 Technological Innovation through Distributed Ledger Mechanism

6.3.1 What Is Technological Innovation

In a fast-paced society, every organization is looking for some technological innovation to increase production or increase the company's profit. Before understanding what technological innovation is, we need first to understand the basic definition of innovation. Innovation can be defined as the incarnation of knowledge that is relatively new into a tool, process or technology.

Sahal [40] defined innovation as an invention that essentially creates a new device. Further, the creation also involves using the newly invented device for commercial purposes or in some application.

According to Girifalco [41], innovation is how an invention is transformed into a usable product. The creation process revolves around continuous improvement and refinement of the product, from starting with the initial design to production of the prototype.

Innovation can be viewed as initiating from a basic idea to the manufacturing of the prototype and product, which finally can be used commercially. Thus, the process includes the invention and implementation, which involves many stages such as research development, production and marketing [42].

Technological progress is not sufficient for the society fit for humans, but it is an essential and necessary component. Now the question is, where does this technological progress come from? A vital distinction to understand between invention and adaption, is that both design and adoption are necessary in the latter. It is essential for a technologist first to conceive a new device, and second, it is required for that device to find use in society. It must be either economically or socially beneficial. Social norms and social technology can facilitate both, where they can preclude both invention and adoption. A society norm and structure can either assist or obstruct both design and adoption. New technologies can quickly be outlawed, such as fire alarms which were banned by the Japanese governments of the 16th, 17th and 18th centuries. The critical requirement for adoption is the recognition of something outside of society.

Technological innovation can be thought of as the accumulation of new knowledge. Thus, the collection of knowledge over time might bring about a creative idea. An innovative idea discovered from the corpus of knowledge might be unique from another existing idea. Converting this unique idea through design, production and, finally, implementation is called innovation (see Figure 6.12). When innovation is in the advancement of an ongoing technology, it is called *technological innovation*. One can say that there is a difference between technology and innovation. Technology focuses on the existing knowledge used in existing tools. In contrast, innovation focuses on the derivation of new knowledge from the existing one and developing a new product based on the existing product. The primary focus of the technological innovation might be in solving problems existing in a business or organization, which might increase the company's productivity, efficiency and reliability, which would help in the growth of the wider economy [43].

In the late 19th and early 20th centuries, technological innovation showed some remarkable growth in Germany's progress with the creation of multiple products [44]. There are different types of technological innovations such as product innovation and process innovation. Product innovation is where a retailer introduces a product to a customer that is distinct from other products. Similarly, process innovation might include new knowledge and new tools, and is used in the backend of manufacturing a particular product

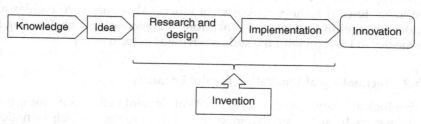

FIGURE 6.12
Technological innovation process.

for service. The main focus of such an innovation is to introduce the newly created product or service into the market. Possible examples of process innovation might include different quality control methods or new ways of delivering a product.

Yang [45] discussed the technological innovations of private enterprise. This author discussed factors for the technological innovation by private enterprise. In order to include technological innovation in private enterprise the first and foremost aspect needed is an innovative idea from the entrepreneur. These innovative ideas might be helpful in different activities such as labor, technology and capital. Technological innovations have gained increaseed attention in the recent past. Innovation is a challenging factor where a company is doing lot of research for launching their product in a unique way to attract customers.

6.3.2 Technological Innovation and Business Model

The business of any firm largely depends upon technology, and changes with the latest technology. New technology can improve the profitability of any firm. It has been noted that business managers and entrepreneurs also focus on how technology is changing regularly. Thus, it can be said that the business model and technology innovation are a two-way and complex process [46]. Therefore, it can be said that technology from any sector, such as information technology, impacts any business model being created, for example, smartwatches are one such example of a technological innovation which is not only used as a watch but also works as a health-monitoring device by monitoring the pulse of the wearer. Another example is smart television which has changed the way that people watch television by interacting with the television and controlling the television content. These technologies have changed the business of every sector, and every business now thinks of new technologies to increase its number of customers and the profit of the company.

All markets are today impacted by digital technology, and it is becoming increasingly difficult to understand and develop products and devices according to the needs of customers because of the shift in the demands of customers toward technology-based products. Also, there are regular and sudden changes in technologies. Therefore, it is increasingly challenging for businesses to keep up with the sudden changes in technology.

6.3.3 Technological Innovation for the Economy

Technological innovation can act as a critical element in the economic growth of any nation. It can be said that innovation is the engine that helps a nation's economic progress, and welfare is an instrument that can be used to solve the current and upcoming global challenges that are impacting the environment and health areas [47]. Rosenberg [48] discussed the two fundamental ways of increasing an economy's output; first, either increase the number of inputs going into the production process, or, second, think differently to get a more significant number of results with the same number of inputs.

Many different studies have shown that using innovative activities widely in technology has achieved increased growth rates [49] in profits as compared to other businesses, which has had a direct impact on employment regardless of the size or other characteristics of the industry. However, if innovation is considered as a significant element in production growth, ironically, it adds concerns about the effects of technological innovation on employment.

With the increase in technological innovation, the quality and variety of products have increased many-fold. Thus, increasing the demand for products in new markets, might give rise to increased income and employment. However, there are always some short-term interruptions with innovation, which might include unsettling some old business models and creating unemployment [50, 51]. For example, if we talk about the economy of Germany, the challenge faced by Germany was in the reduction of labor productivity growth [52]. A study confirmed that the growth rate of labor productivity was declining in Germany; it was seen that labor productivity growth was five times slower in 2013 as compared to the growth rate in 1992. The reason for this was that in 2013 there was rapid involvement of technological innovations, resulting in technology taking the place of human labor [53].

6.3.4 Distributed Ledger Mechanism

A distributed ledger is similar to a database that can be shared, replicated and synchronised with the users of a decentralized network [54]. A distributed ledger contains the records of different types of transactions and is shared with all the network participants.

A distributed ledger technology was developed in 1992 to create a multi-user system that operates under an environment without any central authority [55]. This means the users connected in the network share the same ledger maintained in that network. Since there is no central operator in the distributed ledger technology, any updates or additions of new information that take place are done in all the shared ledgers of the users.

There are many applications that use distributed ledger mechanism. The use of a distributed ledger mechanism in any system provides many benefits to the system. The first and essential benefit is decentralization; with this feature, any network can work without controlling a single authority. All the nodes present on the decentralized network have control over the web. The decentralized part is also beneficial compared to a centralized network in terms of single authority node failure.

The second benefit of the distributed ledger mechanism is confidence and trust; with the blockchain [56] (a form of DLT) greatly helping to create trust between the users of the network. Since all the network users share the updates or additions of new information by any user on the web, the knowledge of any user is visible to all other users. All the users trust other users of the network that their information will not go outside the network. Thus, a high level of confidence and trust among the users is maintained.

Another benefit that the distributed ledger provides is security of the network and data. With blockchain technology, the data can be stored and processed among various users of the web. With distributed ledger technology, it becomes almost impossible to hack into the network or decode the data.

6.3.5 Technological Innovation through a Distributed Ledger

When combined with a business model, technology will benefit not only the business firm but also the economic growth of the nation. The relationship between technology and business has been the topic of debate for a long time. The distributed ledger technology is one of the latest technologies in upcoming digital technologies that could benefit many different sectors, including the business sector, supply chain, healthcare, real estate, etc. Thus, the distributed ledger cannot only be integrated with the relevant business but also other sectors.

The distributed ledger mechanism became popular with one of its crucial applications, i.e. Bitcoin. The concept of Bitcoin came to light in 2008 when Satoshi Nakamoto gave the idea of a cryptocurrency developed under blockchain technology [57], a type of distributed ledger technology. The invention of blockchain technology in the cryptocurrency world was seen as a new kind of technological innovation through the distributed ledger mechanism. Since then, many other cryptocurrencies have come into the market. Many organizations, including banking and finance, healthcare and real estate, are shifting their firms from a traditional database to a more secure, trustable, decentralized and distributed database. This type of technological innovation has made many industries and organizations believe that this technology will increase productivity within the given time period.

Today, we are living in an era of digital currency, or paperless currency. Earlier all payments made from a buyer to a seller were in the form of currency notes. However, now buyers prefer payment through digital currency, either through a debit card or credit card or the latest payment mode, through a mobile phone. However, all these methods of payment have one thing in common, i.e., a bank. So, all the costs do not go directly from the buyer to the seller, but will pass through a bank. What if we have a technology with which a digital payment goes directly to the seller? Well, the answer that the technological innovation through the distributed ledger mechanism has made this possible. The distributed ledger mechanism uses smart contracts by which payments-related transactions can be made between two users of the network.

The smart contract has replaced the formal written agreement made between two parties. A smart contract is self-executable program codes that are executed based on some preconditions in the program. The basic structure of a smart contract could be an if–then function, i.e., **if** a particular condition is met, **then** the transaction is completed between two parties. The smart contract could be helpful in medical situations where, if a patient is admitted to a hospital in the program, the initial payments could be made to the hospital through smart contracts; thus, a patient can be freed from a lengthy process of admission and billing.

The technological innovations for a smart contract and distributed ledger go together. However, distributed ledger technology provides the platform on which a smart contract works; due to this, the concept of the smart contract came into existence [58]. The main challenge with the smart contract is the coding involved while creating a smart contract. The smart contract is generally written in a more advanced language, such as solidity.

In discussing the technological innovation through the distributed ledger mechanism, the major invention was cryptocurrency. Cryptocurrency is a virtual currency based upon cryptographic algorithms. It is one of the most significant innovations that came through the distributed mechanism. There have been multiple cryptocurrencies invented in recent years, such as Bitcoin, Ethereum, Ripple, Litecoin and many more. The most famous of all these was Bitcoin, developed in 2009. The basic principle of the creation of cryptocurrency is that a single user or any node must not accelerate or misuse the production of the cryptocurrency, and only a certain amount of cryptocurrency can be generated through a cryptocurrency system [59]. This process of developing the cryptocurrency is known as *mining*, and users who mine the cryptocurrency are called *miners*. Thus, mining the cryptocurrency is based on blockchain technology, with the miners joining the blockchain network to mine the cryptocurrencies. Blockchain technology is another technological innovation through the distributed ledger mechanism. Blockchain technology is a new technology being developed under distributed ledger technology to bring about new ways to provide a high level of security, immutability and increased efficiency of the system. Blockchain technology started with the invention of cryptocurrency, but the technology has grown greatly and is now being used in many different sectors, thereby increasing economic growth. The innovation of blockchain technology has allowed many industries to fast-pace their work and associations with suppliers and buyers. Blockchain technology works on a P2P platform, thereby connecting every user on a single platform, making it easier for the user to track and connect with other users and make payments on the same blockchain network, eliminating the need for a third party.

The technological innovation through distributed ledger has given many opportunities to users, both directly and indirectly. There might be some more technological innovations coming shortly through the distributed ledger. However, there have been some innovations seen recently with the merger of broadcast technology and other technologies like AI or the IoT. The union of these big technologies with the distributed ledger might bring about a revolution in the world of technology.

6.4   Secure Digital Currency Mechanism Using Bitcoin

In today's world of technology, where almost everything is computer- or Internet-based, one can think of payments being done through a computer and the Internet. The payment made can be in the form of digital currency, virtual currency or cryptocurrencies. A digital currency can also be referred to as electronic currency, or digital money which means cash in digital form, not as physical currency notes or coins. A virtual currency is a more unregulated currency that is created and issued to and by specific members of a virtual network, whereas a cryptocurrency is another form of digital currency which is more cryptographic based to make money more secure, making it impossible to break [60]. Thus, when a payment is received or made by an individual, he or she can only see the digits increasing or decreasing in the account; this way of dealing with costs is called *digital currency*. There are undoubtedly many advantages to using digital currencies. The most significant advantage of digital currencies is the increase in the speed with which cash is transferred from one account to another, with the transfer of funds being just a click away. Therefore, fund transfer using digital money is fast and easy to use, making it an efficient process. Digital currency can be transferred to any account by a computer, tablet or even a mobile phone that has Internet access to any store, any time, from anywhere and without multiple currency conversions.

A digital currency network is a tamper-proof network that is immutable, meaning that no-one can change the network's content. A digital currency network is free from a third party or middle man, such as banks, for the transfer of payments, making this network protected from any kind of fraud or identity theft. Since no credit card or debit card is used to make the payments, there can be no credit or debit card fraud. Thus, with digital currency, there are fewer chances of hacking a centralized server, as in credit card companies, which would reduce the rate of fraud through cards.

Digital currency, the electronic form of physical money, was introduced in 1960. Since then, digital currency has been transformed into a more effortless way to use and quickly transfer currency. The road map of digital money is shown in the table below [61].

1960	In 1960, through the joint effort of IBM and American Airlines, SABRE (Semi-Automated Business Research Environment) was created wherein physical money was transformed into virtual credits using the official telephone line.
1970s	With the arrival of mainframe computer systems, banks started to track funds from one bank to another. This was the era when electronic money came into existence.
1980s	With the introduction of Minitel systems in France, it became easier for customers to pay from home when buying products. Banks like Citibank, Chase, Manhattan, Chemical bank and Manufacturers Hannover offered customers online banking using dial-up connections.
1990s	In this era, the digital currency Digi Cash was invented by David Chaum. This type of digital currency allowed the anonymous transfer of funds. However, few companies and individual were interested in this type of digital currency.
1998	The innovation reached in the era was where electronic money transfer was done through the email addresses of the user with PayPal.
2008	This era was the best of all the eras, with the innovation of digital currency reaching its best phase. Researcher Satoshi Nakamoto in 2008 produced a white paper in which he discussed the digital currency called Bitcoin. The currency was known as cryptocurrency and is somewhat different from digital currency as cryptocurrency is based on a cryptographic algorithm.

6.4.1 What Is Cryptocurrency

A cryptocurrency is a form of digital currency invented in 2008. Cryptocurrencies are slightly different from digital currency as cryptocurrencies are more secure and reliable than simple digital currency. Cryptocurrency was developed under the regulation and environment of cryptography, and cryptographic hash functions more specifically. The cryptographic hash function is a mathematical function. It has three main attributes: the cryptographic hash function can take any string as input and produces a fixed length of output (256 bits for SHA256), and also the hash function should be efficiently computable, meaning that for any size of input, it can produce the work in a reasonable amount of time. To use a cryptographic hash function, the hash function needs to be very secure. Therefore, a question arises as to why cryptocurrency is needed. The answer is to avoid the *double spending problem*.

6.4.2 Double Spending Problem

Double spending involves a cash scheme in which the same single digital token is spent twice or more. This is possible as the digital token consists of a digital file that can be duplicated or falsified. As with counterfeit money, such double-spending creates inflation by creating a new amount of currency that has not existed before that time during the duplication and falsification of the digital file. This process devalues the currency relative to other monitory units. The fundamental cryptographic technique prevents double-spending problem while preserving anonymity of transactioner's blind signature, particularly during offline system secret splitting. The prevention of double spending has taken general forms of centralized and decentralized. This is usually implemented using an online centralized trusted third party to verify if a token has been spent. This usually represents a single point of failure from both the availability and trust viewpoint. By 2007, several distributed systems for double-spend prevention had been proposed. Then, in early 2009, with the arrival of cryptocurrency Bitcoin, a solution was implemented. Bitcoin uses proof-of-work to avoid the need for a trusted third party to timestamp the transactions. All these timestamps are recorded in the public ledger called the blockchain, thereby avoiding double spending.

6.4.3 Bitcoin

Before going into detail of understanding what Bitcoin is, we need to understand what the need for Bitcoin is. First, we need to talk about money. So, what is money exactly? At its core, money represents value. If a person does some work, he will receive money in return; then this money can be used to pay for something from someone else in the future. Throughout history, value has taken many forms, and people have used many different materials to represent money. However, for any other materials in place of money, people need to trust the material. It should be valuable and remain valuable long enough to redeem its value in the future. Since it was challenging to carry valuables all the time, paper money was invented, and banks and government hold this paper money. Therefore, spending paper money was much easier rather than using valuable items. Now that paper money is in use, the value of today's money comes from a legal status given to it by a central authority such as the government. Thus, the trust model has changed from trusting something to trusting someone (government). There are two issues with paper money; one is that it is centralized (there is a central authority that controls and issues it like a government or bank) and second, it is not limited in quantity, which means the government or central authority can print money as much as they want whenever needed, which may inflate the money supply in the market and, as a consequence, the value of money drops.

For this reason, a move to digital money was needed. The move to digital money was pretty simple. Since the central authority issues money, why not make money digital and that authority could keep track of who owns what. Today, people mostly use credit cards, debit cards, PayPal and other forms of digital money, which reduces the amount of physical cash to an almost negligible level.

If a person has a file representing a dollar, then multiple copies can be made for this file generating millions of dollars, which is one form of the double spending problem. The solution that banks use today is a centralized solution. A ledger is kept on a computer, which keeps track of who owns what. Every user has an account, and every ledger has a tally for each account. Thus, the user trusts the bank and the bank trusts the computer, so the solution is centralized in the ledger in the computer. However, the invention of Bitcoin in 2009 provided another way of solving the double spending problem by forming a decentralized network. The Bitcoin was a transparent ledger without a central authority, whereas for a bank, the ledger is not transparent and is centralized. Thus, in a Bitcoin ledger, any user can look into the ledger and view the balance and transactions taking place in the ledger. However, it is impossible to check who is doing the marketing and the owner of the balance in the ledger. This means that *Bitcoin is user anonymous.* Everything in the ledger is open and trackable, but it is not possible to track who is sending what to whom. Since Bitcoin is a decentralized system, there is no single authority of the network. Each computer that participates in the network shares a copy of the ledger, also known as the *blockchain.*

Unlike a physical currency, a bitcoin is a digital currency, meaning there are no physical coins available, only rows of transactions and balances. When a person owns a Bitcoin, that means that the person holds the right to access a specific Bitcoin address record in the ledger and can send funds from this record to a different address. Thus, Bitcoin is the new Internet of money that is offers a decentralized solution to money. There are many advantages to Bitcoin over the current system. First, Bitcoin gives the user complete control over their money. Only users have the authority to access the currency, which means no government or central authority has permission to block the user's account.

Second, Bitcoin also removes the middlemen from transferring the money. This means that Bitcoin is much cheaper than physical money for the process of money orders.

Third, unlike paper currency, bitcoin was designed to be digital by nature, meaning that an additional layer of programming can be added on top of it, which could turn it into smart money, also known as *smart contracts.*

Finally, Bitcoin opens up digital commerce to about 2.5 billion people who do not have access to the current banking system. These people are unbanked or underbanked, maybe because of the place they live in. However, with a smartphone and Internet connection, these people can also trade in Bitcoin without any permission needed from any authority as some Bitcoin networks are open to anyone (these networks are known as the public blockchain network). Several merchants accept Bitcoin as a digital currency, including Microsoft, Expedia and Wikipedia.

6.4.4 Bitcoin Mining

Bitcoin was created as a decentralized alternative to the banking system. This means that the system can transfer funds from one account to another without any central authority. The central authority transferring funds is relatively easy, just information to the bank to transfer the amount from one account to another. In this case, the bank has the authority to do this as only the bank has the ledger, which holds the balances to update the version for everyone in the system. Thus, a decentralized system was invented where the sender can directly transfer the funds to the receiver without any bank or central authority intervention. The rules applied in the Bitcoin system protocol solve this issue in a very creative and efficient manner. Anyone can participate in Bitcoin's mining process as the process is open to anyone in the network or wishing to join the network. To mine a Bitcoin, the user has to predict a random number. The computer system makes this prediction of the random number. The more fast and powerful the system, the faster are the guesses of this random number per second; if the user manages to guess the correct random number, they earn a Bitcoin and get on the next page of the Bitcoin transaction on the blockchain.

Let's now discuss the mining process in a bit more detail. Once your mining computer comes up with the right guess, the mining program determines which of the current pending transactions will be grouped into the next block of transactions. The block created and the solution for finding the correct random number are sent to the whole of the blockchain network so that other computers present on the web can validate the new transaction. Each computer on the network that validates the solution updates its copy of the Bitcoin transaction ledger present locally on the computers with the trade that has been chosen to be included in the next block.

Since mining is based on guessing for each block, any miner can guess the correct number and get access to update the blockchain. It is a fact that a miner having greater computing power will succeed more often. However, due to the law of statistical probability, it is doubtful that every miner will go to do the same job again and again. Also, when this stage is completed, the system generates a fixed number of Bitcoins. The user receives the reward as compensation for the time and energy spent in solving the mathematical problem. In addition to this, the user also gets paid any transaction fees attached to the transactions inserted into the block. Thus, this process helps in mining new Bitcoins from the system created.

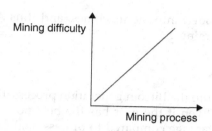

FIGURE 6.13
Mining process.

Satoshi Nakamoto who invented the Bitcoin has applied some rules for mining in such a way that the greater the mining power of the network, the more difficult it is to guess the solution to the problem for mining.

Therefore, the difficulty of the mining process is self-adjusting to accumulate the mining power that the network possesses. If more miners join the network, the difficulty level of the problem also increases and it becomes more challenging to solve the problem (see Figure 6.13). If some of the miners leave the grid the difficulty level decreases, making it easier for them to solve it. This is known as *mining difficulty*. Thus, the motive of Satoshi Nakamoto was to create a steady flow of new Bitcoins to the system, which could also keep inflation in check. The mining difficulty is set so that only 10 new blocks (average) are added each minute.

When mining Bitcoins started in 2009 there were not many miners ess and mining a Bitcoin was straightforward with a simple computer having an average speed and power since the mining difficulty was very low. However, as Bitcoin started to gain more users, people started looking for more powerful mining solutions and moved on to GPU mining. A GPU or graphics processing unit is a unique component added to computers to carry out more complex calculations. GPU is designed for the gamers to run computer games with intense graphics requirements. Because of GPU's architecture, these devices have become popular in cryptography, and, in 2011, users started using GPU for mining Bitcoins. It should be noted that the mining power of 1 GPU = 30 CPU. Another revolution in mining came after GPU with FPGA (field programmable gate array) mining. FPGA is a piece of computer hardware that can be connected to a computer to run a set of calculations. FPGA is similar to GPU, but three to 100 times faster. The disadvantage with FPGA is that they are harder to configure. This is the reason it is not as successful as GPU in the mining process.

Finally, in 2013, a new set of miners came into existence, "ASIC Miners." ASIC stands for application-specific integrated circuits. These pieces of hardware were explicitly created for mining Bitcoin. In contrast to to CPU, GPU and FPGA, ASIC could not be used for any other purpose. The functions of ASIC were hardcoded into the machines, and thus ASIC miners are the current standard for mining.

6.4.5 Mining Pools

When a user enters into the Bitcoin generation process, the user is up against heavy competition. Even if the user has the best possible miners, the user might have a disadvantage compared to professional Bitcoin mining farms. That is where the Bitcoin mining poll came into existence. A mining pool is nothing but a collection of miners grouped together, where they combine their mining powers to compete faster and more efficiently. If the pool manages to win the competition, the reward is spread out among all pool miners depending upon how much mining power the individual has contributed. In this way, even small miners can join the mining game and generate Bitcoin. However, small miners sometimes need to pay a small fee for rendering their services. Today, over a dozen large pools compete for the chance to mine Bitcoin and update their ledgers.

6.4.6 Blockchain Process

A blockchain process is based on the consensus mechanism for a transaction to be verified and valid (see Figure 6.14). A blockchain network consists of various nodes connected in a distributed and decentralized fashion. Any node that needs to perform a transaction has to write the transaction in a block. A block can be thought of as a container-like data structure that can consist of about 500 transactions on average; however, the size of a block can

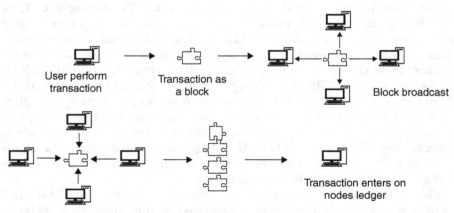

FIGURE 6.14
Blockchain process.

be up to 1 MB [62]. The node performs a transaction in a block and this is sent to other nodes connected in a distributed network. Since the blockchain network is decentralized, the block of marketing is created by the node; hence the block is broadcast to all the nodes present in the network. The blockchain network is a consensus-based network, meaning all the nodes present have to agree on the transaction made based on a consensus algorithm. A consensus algorithm is a process by which multiple nodes present in a distributed network agreed upon a decision [63]. The consensus algorithm provides reliability to a distributed network. There are many consensus algorithms; some include *Proof of Work, Proof of stake, Byzantine Fault Tolerance* and many others. Thus, a block created is added to the blocks already present in the blockchain once it is verified and validated by all the nodes present in the network, as shown in the figure. The newly added block will always refer to the previous block in the chain, which will make the chain more secure. Once the block is added to the chain of blocks, the receiver node can update the ledger with the new information.

6.4.7 Consensus Algorithms

So far, we have described what a blockchain is; It is a distributed ledger. Consider a situation where we have five mining nodes, all the nodes will have a copy of the blockchain, and all the documents will be of the same state, which means all the nodes will have exact copies. Now this network receives a new block after making some transactions. This new block needs to be added to the blockchain. But then, which mining node will add this block into the blockchain? The last node must add the latest block into the blockchain, but the problem here is if the latest node in the blockchain is a malicious node [64]. Here the question is how the decision is made to add a new node. Therefore, all the nodes agree upon a decision whether to add the new block into the blockchain or not. The process by which a group of nodes makes some decision and all the individual nodes agree upon and support the conclusion gives the best solution, whcich is known as the consensus process [65]. Multiple algorithms come under this consensus process called *consensus algorithms.*

6.4.8 Types of Consensus Algorithms

There are many consensus algorithms that are roughly divided into two categories: proof-based and BFT-based.

In a proof-based consensus mechanism, the network leader is selected randomly out of many other nodes and suggests the final value. This type of consensus algorithms is also termed a *permissionless algorithm* [66]. Proof of work was one such mechanism useful in mining the Bitcoin and Ethereum cryptocurrencies. Proof-based algorithms consist of proof of work, proof of stake and delegated proof of stake.

In the BFT-based version (Byzantine fault tolerance), the network leader is elected through multiple rounds of voting between the nodes of the network [67]. This type of consensus mechanism is also known as a *consortium or permissioned consensus mechanism*.

6.4.9   Proof of Work

The basic idea behind this was first introduced in 1993 to combat spam emails, and was formally called the proof of work [68] in 1997. However, the technique went largely unused until Satoshi Nakamoto created Bitcoin in 2009. He realized that this mechanism could be used to reach consensus between many nodes on a network, and he used it to secure the Bitcoin blockchain. The proof of work algorithm works by having all nodes solve a cryptographic puzzle [69].

A proof of work protocol is a vehicle by which someone can effectively prove that they have engaged in a significant amount of computational effort. Proof of work protocols often amount to puzzles, and these puzzles can be very challenging to solve, which means these puzzles require severe computational effort, and there are no short cuts for this [70]. On the other hand, that effort can be easily verified in significantly less time than it took to conduct in the first place. There are many numbers of applications that use POW, and Bitcoin is one of them. In any timestamp network, the proof of work can be implemented by incrementing the values of the nonce [71]. A nonce is a field in the block, usually an arbitrary or random number, used in cryptography as protection against a reply attack. The value of the nonce should be unique for each block and can be used only once. The value of nonce is appended to the end of whatever is intended to hash. Thus, if somebody tries to reuse the same notes, it will lead to failure as each letter must be unique. Each time the user tries to attempt modification and the user has used that node, then blockchain will get distrubed. When mining a Bitcoin using proof of work, it will ask to answer the puzzle and the letters.

The proof of work can also help determine representation in the majority of decision-making. But if the majority is based on *one-IP-address one vote*, then it is possible that anyone could disrupt this and allocate many IP addresses. Here comes the idea behind proof of work, where the majority is based on *one CPU one vote*. In this, the decision taken by the majority is based on the representation of the longest chain where the highest proof of work effort is devoted.

The biggest problem with the proof of work is the amount of electricity used and the amount of energy wasted, which is terrible for the environment. It encourages the use of mining pools which makes the blockchain more centralized as opposed to decentralized. According to *Digiconomist*, Bitcoin miners alone uses about 54 TWh of electricity, enough to power 5 million households in the USA or even to supply all of New Zealand. For the PoW, a computer needs to have a lot of processing power for which additional peripherals are also necessary, which incurs extra cost. With the mining process of PoW, the mining would get more complicated when the amount of Bitcoin decreases or it is less available. Therefore, some miners decided to mine another digital currency known as Ethereum, which uses pProof of stake.

6.4.10 Proof of Stake

Bitcoin uses an enormous amount of energy to secure its network, and mining new coins needs a lot of computing power because of the proof of work algorithm. Therefore, there have to be some other alternatives other than cryptocurrency. In 2011, a Bitcointalk forum user called QantumMechanic proposed a technique called "proof of stake." The basic idea behind proof of stake was that competing against one another with mining is wasteful. Instead of this, the proof of stake uses an election process in which only one node is randomly chosen to validate the next block. Unlike proof of work, there are no miners in proof of stake; instead, they are called validators, and it does not let people mine a new block but instead they "mint" or "forge" new block and the process is called minting or forging.

To become a validator, one node has to deposit several coins in the network as a stake, something like a security deposit. The size of the stakes determines the chances of a validator being chosen to forge the next block. Although this might not look fair because electing a validator favors the rich, in reality, it is more appropriate as compared to proof of work. With proof of work, the affluent users can enjoy the benefits and power of economics at scale. The price the user pays for mining equipment and the electricity does not go up linearly; instead, the more they buy, the better their prices. However, in proof of stake, if the node is chosen to validate the next block, the user will check if all the transactions are valid. If everything checks out, the node signs off on the block and adds it to the blockchain, and as a reward, the node will receive the fees associated with each transaction. But now the question arises as to how the validators can be trusted on the network. That's where the role stakes come in; the validators will lose a part of their stake if they approve any fraudulent transaction; as long as the stakes of the validator are higher than what the validators get from the transaction fees, it would prove that the validators are correctly doing their job, and if not they will lose more money compared to what they gain. This is a financial motivator and holds up as long as the stakes are higher than the sum of all transaction fees. If any node stops being a validator, his stake and all the transaction fees that he has received will be released after a certain period after discovering that some of the blocks were fraudulent.

6.4.11 Difference between Proof of Work (PoW) and Proof of Stake (PoS)

Proof of stake does not let everyone mine for new blocks and, therefore, uses considerably less energy and is more decentralized. In proof of work, there is something called mining pools, where the users team up to increase their chances of mining a new block and thus collecting the rewards. However, these pools can control a large portion of the Bitcoin blockchain. They centralize the mining process, which is quite dangerous. If, let says three to four mining pools merge, they would have the majority stake in the network and the possibility that they could start approving fraudulent transactions. This type of problem is known as a 51% attack.

Another most important advantage is that setting up a node for a proof of stake-based blockchain is much less expensive as compared to for a proof of work-based one. There is absolutely no need for expensive mining equipment. Thus, proof of stake encourages more users to set up a node and make the network more decentralized and secure. However, even proof of stake isn't perfect and has some flaws. For example, if a user buys a majority of the stake in a network, that user can effectively control the web and approve fake transactions (51% attack).

Proof of stake also has to be very careful when selecting the following validators. This cannot be random because the size of the stake has to be factored in. Still, at the same time, the stake alone isn't enough because that will favor more affluent users, who will be chosen more frequently and will collect more transactions fees and, in turn, become more affluent, which again increases the chance of them being selected as a validator even more often.

Another potential problem is when the network chooses the next validator, but the user does not come up for this job; it then selects a large number of backup validators as a fallback.

Peercoin, Lisk and Nxt are some of the coins that use the proof of stake algorithm as a mining algorithm. Ethereum, for example, is working on implementing a proof of stake system called *Casper*. It is currently deployed on the Ethereum test net and is actively being developed.

6.4.12 Delegated Proof of Stake

Delegated proof of stake (DPoS) is another consensus algorithm used in blockchain-based networks to determine the validator of each block and after a consensus decision is made on what data should be added to the chain.

The DPoS was invented in 2013 by Dan Larimer while solving issues related to Bitcoin's proof of work. Initially, the DPoS was created to power the cryptocurrency BitShare. DPoS is delegated through the stake in a new consensus algorithm that allows the shareholders of the system to have control over who is certifying the ledger. This will enable the user to have 10 seconds block time to process transactions at 10 seconds per transaction or more and allow the network to scale to have dedicated nodes that are highly efficient specialized yet remain in the control of the shareholders. Therefore, we can have the 10-second confirmation on the block, which is securer than Bitcoin. Also, the delegated proof of stake user appoints someone else to secure the network on their behalf, and these would be the delegates. There are 101 delegates, who take turns to randomly produce blocks, say every 10 seconds.

The most significant disadvantage with both the proof of work and proof of stake is that they are both vulnerable to 51% attack and 51% shareholder attack, respectively. However, there is nothing that can avoid the 51% attack since it is part of the inherent nature of a consensus algorithm. The cost incurred in proof of work is however much higher than in any other system for acquiring a 51% attack.

The DPoS is much faster than any other system because DPoS uses a deterministic manner of producing blocks that don't have to rely on random chance. The delegates are well-proven nodes that the shareholder knows and they have dedicated high reliability to make a block every 10 seconds but with no variability, unlike other systems. Due to the way the system works, the user has complete confirmation of almost zero likelihood of any blockchain faults in just 10 seconds. Therefore, DPoS is fast and secure, and less centralized.

6.4.13 Byzantine Fault Tolerance (BLT)

The BFT consensus algorithm is based on a prevalent problem known as the Byzantine gGeneral problem. The Byzantine general problem is a question of consensus. Mountains and other barriers surrounded the generals; these generals can communicate only by sending messengers. In addition to this, they had not decided before whether to attack the city or to give up and retreat. Now, only after observing the enemy, do they agree on a joint plan of action. Only an attack launched by all generals at once can successfully conquer the city. Having gone this far, they send the messenger with their votes on how to proceed. However, the problem is that some of the generals may have been bribed. In exchange for their betrayal, they will earn themselves a small fortune from the city. These traitor generals will provide incorrect information to their peers to foil the attack and prevent consensus. Also, their messengers could get lost or corrupt their messages. The question here arises as to how peace can then be achieved. Again, there is no solution in the presence of one-third or a higher percentage of potential traitor generals. These traitor generals are known as the Byzantine nodes, and they may act maliciously or arbitrarily.

Practical Byzantine Fault Tolerance, released in 1993 by Miguel Castro and Barbara Liskov, gives an algorithm to allow nodes to reach a consensus with no more than one-third Byzantine nodes. This paper has inspired many iterations of Byzantine fault tolerance algorithms, especially as research into the blockchain consensus algorithm. Let's now see the various types of faults within distributed systems. There are mainly two types of responsibility possible. The first type of fault is a fail-stop fault. During a fail-stop mark, the node can crash or not return values. Recall that a node functionally includes sending, receiving, storing and processing information. Early research into distributed consensus first aimed to solve these kinds of problems. This kind of failure may be temporary or indefinite, but it will always be more easy to handle than the second type of fault. A Byzantine fault, referring to the Byzantine generals problem, is a fault that refers to any arbitrary deviance from the protocol. This means not only that the nodes might stop replying or receiving information, but they may also send corrupted and false information. The Byzantine faults are a superset of fail-stop defects. The behavior of most attackers, such as the bribed generals trying to hinder consensus, falls under this kind of fault. This type of fault is one that all public blockchains must protect against since the participants in the blockchain network are unknown and unpredictable.

References

1. Cicirelli, Franco, Antonio Guerrieri, Giandomenico Spezzano, and Andrea Vinci (2017). An edge-based platform for dynamic smart city applications. *Future Generation Computer Systems, 76,* 106–118.
2. Yucel, Sakir (2017). Smart city wireless platforms for smart cities. *In Proceedings of the International Conference on Modeling, Simulation and Visualization Methods (MSV),* pp. 100–106. The Steering Committee of the World Congress in Computer Science, Computer Engineering and Applied Computing (WorldComp).
3. Peng, Wei, Wei Gao, and Jiajia Liu (2019). AI-enabled massive devices multiple access for smart city. *IEEE Internet of Things Journal, 6*(5), 7623–7634.
4. Silva, Bhagya Nathali, Murad Khan, and Kijun Han (2018). Towards sustainable smart cities: A review of trends, architectures, components, and open challenges in smart cities. *Sustainable Cities and Society, 38,* 697–713.
5. Rusti, Bogdan, Horia Stefanescu, Marius Iordache, Jean Ghenta, Catalin Brezeanu, and Cristian Patachia (2019). Deploying Smart City components for 5G network slicing. In *2019 European Conference on Networks and Communications (EuCNC),* pp. 149–154. IEEE.
6. Barbosa, José, Paulo Leitão, Damien Trentesaux, Armando W. Colombo, and Stamatis Karnouskos (2016). Cross benefits from cyber-physical systems and intelligent products for future smart industries. In *2016 IEEE 14th International Conference on Industrial Informatics (INDIN),* pp. 504–509. IEEE.
7. Koresh, M. H. J. D., and Deva, J. (2019). Computer vision based traffic sign sensing for smart transport. *Journal of Innovative Image Processing (JIIP), 1*(01), 11–19.

8. Biswas, Kamanashis, and Vallipuram Muthukkumarasamy (2016). Securing smart cities using blockchain technology. In *2016 IEEE 18th International Conference on High Performance Computing and Communications; IEEE 14th International Conference on Smart City; IEEE 2nd International Conference on Data Science and Systems (HPCC/SmartCity/DSS)*, pp. 1392–1393. IEEE.

9. Jiang, Li, Shengli Xie, Sabita Maharjan, and Yan Zhang (2019). Blockchain empowered wireless power transfer for green and secure Internet of Things. *IEEE Network, 33*(6), 164–171.

10. Nam, Kichan, Christopher S. Dutt, Prakash Chathoth, and M. Sajid Khan (2019). Blockchain technology for smart city and smart tourism: Latest trends and challenges. *Asia Pacific Journal of Tourism Research, 26*(4), 454–468.

11. Hakak, Saqib, Wazir Zada Khan, Gulshan Amin Gilkar, Muhammad Imran, and Nadra Guizani (2020). Securing smart cities through blockchain technology: Architecture, requirements, and challenges. *IEEE Network, 34*(1), 8–14.

12. Batubara, F. Rizal, Jolien Ubacht, and Marijn Janssen (2018). Challenges of blockchain technology adoption for e-government: A systematic literature review. In *Proceedings of the 19th Annual International Conference on Digital Government Research: Governance in the Data Age*, pp. 1–9.

13. Butt, Shariq Aziz, Jorge Luis Diaz-Martinez, Tauseef Jamal, Arshad Ali, Emiro De-La-Hoz-Franco, and Muhammad Shoaib (2019). IoT Smart Health Security Threats. In *2019 19th International Conference on Computational Science and Its Applications (ICCSA)*, pp. 26–31. IEEE.

14. Mahmoud, Rwan, Tasneem Yousuf, Fadi Aloul, and Imran Zualkernan (2015). Internet of things (IoT) security: Current status, challenges and prospective measures. In *2015 10th International Conference for Internet Technology and Secured Transactions (ICITST)*, pp. 336–341. IEEE.

15. Singh, Sushil Kumar, Shailendra Rathore, and Jong Hyuk Park (2020). BlockIoTintelligence: A blockchain-enabled intelligent IoT architecture with artificial intelligence. *Future Generation Computer Systems, 110*, 721–743.

16. Gharbieh, Mohammad, Hesham ElSawy, Ahmed Bader, and Mohamed-Slim Alouini (2017). Spatiotemporal stochastic modeling of IoT enabled cellular networks: Scalability and stability analysis. *IEEE Transactions on Communications, 65*(8), 3585–3600.

17. Kodali, Ravi Kishore, Vishal Jain, Suvadeep Bose, and Lakshmi Boppana (2016). IoT based smart security and home automation system. In *2016 international conference on computing, communication and automation (ICCCA)*, pp. 1286–1289. IEEE.

18. Nilsson, Nils J. (2014). *Principles of Artificial Intelligence*. California, USA: Morgan Kaufmann.

19. Adhikari, Pashupati R., and Reza Mirshams (2017). Study of knowledge-based system (KBS) and decision making methodologies in materials selection for lightweight aircraft metallic structures. *Journal of Applied Science & Engineering Technology, 5*(1), 1.

20. Azar, Ahmad Taher, and Sundarapandian Vaidyanathan (Eds.) (2015). *Computational Intelligence Applications in Modeling and Control*. Switzerland, Europe: Springer International Publishing.

21. Chen, Wei, Mahdi Panahi, Paraskevas Tsangaratos, Himan Shahabi, Ioanna Ilia, Somayeh Panahi, Shaojun Li, Abolfazl Jaafari, and Baharin Bin Ahmad

(2019). Applying population-based evolutionary algorithms and a neuro-fuzzy system for modeling landslide susceptibility. *Catena, 172*, 212–231.

22. Kramer, Oliver (2017). *Genetic Algorithm Essentials*. Vol. 679. Oldenburg, Germany: Springer.

23. Demuth, Howard B., Mark H. Beale, Orlando De Jess, and Martin T. Hagan (2014). *Neural Network Design*. USA: Martin Hagan.

24. Van Gerven, Marcel, and Sander Bohte (2017). Artificial neural networks as models of neural information processing. *Frontiers in Computational Neuroscience, 11*, 114.

25. Xiao, Liang, Xiaoyue Wan, Xiaozhen Lu, Yanyong Zhang, and Di Wu (2018). IoT security techniques based on machine learning: How do IoT devices use AI to enhance security?. *IEEE Signal Processing Magazine, 35*(5), 41–49.

26. Vakula, D., and Bandari Raviteja (2017). Smart public transport for smart cities. In *2017 International Conference on Intelligent Sustainable Systems (ICISS)*, pp. 805–810. IEEE.

27. Shyam, Gopal Kirshna, Sunilkumar S. Manvi, and Priyanka Bharti (2017). Smart waste management using Internet-of-Things (IoT). In *2017 2nd International Conference on Computing and Communications Technologies (ICCCT)*, pp. 199–203. IEEE.

28. Tsiropoulou, Eirini Eleni, John S. Baras, Symeon Papavassiliou, and Surbhit Sinha (2017). RFID-based smart parking management system. *Cyber-Physical Systems, 3*(1–4), 22–41.

29. Sheth, Amit (2016). Internet of things to smart IoT through semantic, cognitive, and perceptual computing. *IEEE Intelligent Systems, 31*(2), 108–112.

30. Banerjee, Amit, Chinmay Chakraborty, Anand Kumar, and Debabrata Biswas (2020). Emerging trends in IoT and big data analytics for biomedical and health care technologies. In *Handbook of Data Science Approaches for Biomedical Engineering*, pp. 121–152. USA: Academic Press.

31. Hassanalieragh, Moeen, Alex Page, Tolga Soyata, Gaurav Sharma, Mehmet Aktas, Gonzalo Mateos, Burak Kantarci, and Silvana Andreescu (2015). Health monitoring and management using Internet-of-Things (IoT) sensing with cloud-based processing: Opportunities and challenges. In *2015 IEEE International Conference on Services Computing*, pp. 285–292. IEEE.

32. Zhou, Guoxu, Qibin Zhao, Yu Zhang, Tülay Adalı, Shengli Xie, and Andrzej Cichocki (2016). Linked component analysis from matrices to high-order tensors: Applications to biomedical data. *Proceedings of the IEEE, 104*(2), 310–331.

33. Singh, Mandeep (2014). *Introduction to Biomedical Instrumentation*. New Delhi, India: PHI Learning Pvt. Ltd..

34. Gao, Lan, Li Xia, Song-Qing Pan, Tao Xiong, and Shu-Chuen Li (2015). Burden of epilepsy: A prevalence-based cost of illness study of direct, indirect and intangible costs for epilepsy. *Epilepsy Research, 110*, 146–156.

35. Katare, Geetanjali, Gourish Padihar, and Z. Quereshi (2018). Challenges in the integration of artificial intelligence and Internet of things. *International Journal of System and Software Engineering, 6*(2), 10–15.

36. Sodhro, Ali Hassan, Sandeep Pirbhulal, and Arun Kumar Sangaiah (2018). Convergence of IoT and product lifecycle management in medical health care. *Future Generation Computer Systems, 86*, 380–391.

37. Shah, Rushabh, and Alina Chircu (2018). IoT and AI in healthcare: a systematic literature review. *Issues in Information Systems, 19*(3), 33–41.
38. Patel, Mitesh S., David A. Asch, and Kevin G. Volpp (2015). Wearable devices as facilitators, not drivers, of health behavior change. *Jama, 313*(5), 459–460.
39. Cánovas-Segura, Bernardo, Manuel Campos, Antonio Morales, Jose M. Juarez, and Francisco Palacios (2016). Development of a clinical decision support system for antibiotic management in a hospital environment. *Progress in Artificial Intelligence, 5*(3), 181–197.
40. Sahal, D. (1997). The multidimentional diffusion of technology. *Technological Forecasting, 10*, 277–298.
41. Girifalco, L. A. (n.d.). *Dynamics of Technological Change*. Van Nostrand Reinhold, New York.
42. Taggart, M. M. (1994). Managing technology and innovation: A review. *R&D Management, 24*(4), 341–353.
43. Diaconu, M. (2011). Technological innovation: Concept, process, typology and implications in the economy. *Theoretical and Applied Economics, XVIII*(10(563)) 127–144.
44. Wim Naudé, P. N. (2017). *Technological Innovation and Inclusive Growth in Germany*. IZA—Institute of Labor Economics.
45. Huan-chun Yang, H. (2011). A study on the technological innovation system and development of private enterprises. *International Conference on Electronics, Communications and Control (ICECC)*, pp. 3042–3045. IEEE.
46. Charles Baden-Fuller, S. H. (2013). *Business models and technological innovation. Science Direct Long Range Planning Journal, 46*(6), 419–426.
47. Diaconu, M. (2011). Technological Innovation:Concept, Process, Typology and Implications in the Economy. *Theoretical and Applied Economics, XVIII*(10(563)), 127–144.
48. Rosenberg, N. (2004). *Innovation And Economic Growth. Organisation for Economic Co-operation and Development*.
49. ÇalÖúkan, H. K. (2015). Technological change and economic growth. *World Conference on Technology, Innovation and Entrepreneurship*, pp. 649–654. ScienceDirect.
50. Kristina Matuzeviciute, M. B. (2017). Do technological innovations affect unemployment? Some empirical evidence from European countries. *Economies, 5*(4), 48—Open Access Journal.
51. James Broughel, A. T. (March 4, 2019). *Technological Innovation and Economic Growth*. Available at: www.mercatus.org: www.mercatus.org/publications/entrepreneurship/technological-innovation-and-economic-growth
52. McGuckin, R. H., Streitwieser, M. L., and Doms, M. (1998). The effect of technology use on productivity growth. *Economics of Innovation and New Technology, 7*(1), 1–26.
53. Witte, K. (December 19, 2017). *Technological Innovation: The Challenges for Labour*. Available at: https://doc-research.org; https://doc-research.org/2017/12/technological-innovation-challenges-labour/
54. Sloane Brakeville, B. P. (June 1, 2019). *Blockchain Basics: Introduction to Distributed Ledgers*. Available at: https://developer.ibm.com/; https://developer.ibm.com/tutorials/cl-blockchain-basics-intro-bluemix-trs/

55. Michel Rauchs, A. G. (2018). *Distributed Ledger Technology Systems: A Conceptual Framework*. SSRN Electronic Journal.

56. Claudia Loebbecke, L. L. (2018). Blockchain technology impacting the role of trust in transactions: Reflections in the case of trading diamonds. *Twenty-Sixth European Conference on Information Systems (ECIS2018)*. Portsmouth, UK.

57. Nakamoto, S. (2009). *Bitcoin: A Peer-to-Peer Electronic Cash System*. Available at: http://citeseerx.ist.psu.edu; http://citeseerx.ist.psu.edu/viewdoc/summary?doi=10.1.1.221.9986

58. ISDA (August 2017). *Smart Contracts and Distributed Ledger—A Legal Perspective*. Available at: www.isda.org; www.isda.org/a/6EKDE/smart-contracts-and-distributed-ledger-a-legal-perspective.pdf

59. Vejačka, M. (2014). Basic Aspects of Cryptocurrencies. *Journal of Economy, Business and Financing*, 2, 75–83.

60. Rose, C. (2015). The Evolution Of Digital Currencies: Bitcoin, A Cryptocurrency Causing A Monetary Revolution. *International Business & Economics Research Journal*, 4, 617.

61. Biggs, J. W. (May 7, 2018). *Introduction to Digital Currency*. Available at: https://bookdown.org; https://bookdown.org/Jack_Biggs/Cryptocurrency/

62. Madeira, A. (November 29, 2016). *What is the Block Size Limit*. Available at: www.cryptocompare.com; www.cryptocompare.com/coins/guides/what-is-the-block-size-limit/

63. Rouse, M. (August 2017). *Consensus Algorithm*. Available at: whatis.techtarget.com; https://whatis.techtarget.com/definition/consensus-algorithm

64. Wei She, Q. L. (2019). *Blockchain Trust Model for Malicious Node Detection in Wireless Sensor Networks*. Special Section on Mobile Service Computing with Internet of Things, pp. 38947–38956. IEEE Access.

65. Anwar, H. (August 25, 2018). *Consensus Algorithms: The Root of the Blockchain Technology*. Available at: https://101blockchains.com/; https://101blockchains.com/consensus-algorithms-blockchain/

66. Baliga, D. A. (2017). *Understanding Blockchain Consensus Models*. Pune, India: Persistent Systems Ltd.

67. Wenbo Wang, D. T. (2018). A survey on consensus mechanisms and mining strategy management in blockchain networks. *arXiv*.

68. Cynthia Dwork, M. N. (2001). Pricing via processing or combatting junk mail. *Annual International Cryptology Conference*, pp. 139–147. Berlin, Heidelberg: Springer.

69. Taotao Li, P. A. (2017). *Designing Proof of Transaction Puzzles for Cryptocurrency*. Cryptology ePrint Archive.

70. Pawel Szalachowski, D. R. (2019). *StrongChain: Transparent and collaborative proof-of-work consensus*. *28th USENIX Security Symposium*, pp. 819–836. Santa Clara, CA, USA: USENIX Association.

71. Alexander Chepurnoy, T. D.-S. (2017). TwinsCoin: A cryptocurrency via proof-of-work and proof-of-stake. *Cryptology ePrint Archive*.

7

Revolution of the Digital World by Strategic Technology Trends

The digital revolution arrived with the advancement of technology from analogue electronics devices to mechanical devices. The process that was started in the 1980s today has reached the most advanced digital technologies and is still on-going. The revolution started over 30 years ago, and was also called the digital process, and was marked as the starting phase of the information era. The first digital revolution started in early 1947 when the transistor was invented for data transfer devices [1]; since then, the digital process has advanced greatly in many different sectors. The digital revolution has played an essential role in the economic growth of all countries. Over the past decade, the digital process has increased its pace with new technologies coming in; therefore organizations have had to adopt these new technologies to increase their production, customer satisfaction, and most importantly, automated the process of incoming and outgoing items, this is a payment or manufacturing of products. The technologies like artificial intelligence, the Internet of Things, and blockchain have received a positive response from society. Many organizations, industries and other sectors have obtained benefits from these new technologies. Since data are very valuable today, these technologies have helped many organizations gather valuable data, analyze the data, and provide privacy and security. With the digital revolution, not only the data but also the currency we use have moved to a digital platform [2]. Cryptocurrency is one type of digital currency generated and used for payments [3]. With the invention of cryptocurrency, the user is not dependent on a central authority for currency generation. The user can generate any cryptocurrency and use this form of digital currency to buy and sell any product or make payments to an individual.

There are many use cases available for technologies like artificial intelligence, the Internet of Things, and blockchain. These use claims either are already implemented and provide benefits to society or are in the process of implementation. Hence, the digital revolution makes devices intelligent and offers good security and privacy for the users of these devices [4].

DOI: 10.1201/9781003046462-8

7.1   Use of Case Studies and Technical Hurdles in AI, the IoT and Blockchain for a New Revolution

7.1.1   Artificial Intelligence in Agriculture

Agriculture has always been a primary source of income in many countries, and all farmer wants to cultivate the best crop so they can obtain the best price. Farmers are engaged in multiple technologies. There is a considerable gap in the technology, and there can be a massive loss of food just because of a simple mistake. Complex situations constantly challenge the farmers, who need to take diligent care of their crops. These devices are described as sensing, as they need to know what is happening and the real needs of the crops. So, where does artificial intelligence fit in with agriculture?

AI can provide some benefits, especially in the thinking process, or we could also say that AI is a digital thinking friend.

The data processing and action where data can be gathered by most recent technology, the processing of data is the thinking, and this is where most of the artificial intelligence comes into action [5]. So, what are the benefits of AI in agriculture? AI can be beneficial in seed breeding [6], which is the selection of seeds, requiring millions of genes to be identified to find the best source for that specific condition. This can be done by artificial intelligence on behalf of the farmer. Artificial intelligence could also be beneficial in checking the fertility of the soil [7]. Many companies are providing services and products based on artificial intelligence.

There are some challenges associated with artificial intelligence which slow down the processes [8]:

1. The availability of the data, if there is no data input, there will be no data output and hence no artificial intelligence.

2. The data quality because if the gathered data are pure junk, then the creation received would also be pure junk in digital terms.

3. The policies and regulation associated with the devices based on artificial intelligence.

7.1.2   Artificial Intelligence in Healthcare

This age of technology knows no bounds. At one time AI was thought to be a futuristic threat to humankind. AI is now changing and saving lives, and is not intended to replace clinicians or clinical judgment. AI serves the purpose of enhancing and complementing the very human interaction between a provider and patient [9]. In healthcare, AI is a game changer with its applications, decision support image analysis, and patient triage to reduce the variations and duplicate testing. Decision support systems can quickly decipher a large amount of data within an electronic medical record [10]. AI technology is also taking the uncertainty out of viewing patient scans by highlighting the problem areas on the images, aiding in the screening and diagnosis process [11]. AI helps with the issue of physician burnout by collecting the patient's data through a mobile app, or some text messaging chat BOTS now ask patients a series of questions regarding their symptoms, on the basis of these symptoms, the BOTs carry out self-diagnosis based on some guesswork, thus saving the time, money and effort of both the patient and provider [12]. With AI integration becoming more innovative it enables solutions to various issues for patients, hospitals and the healthcare industry.

7.1.3   Artificial Intelligence in Finance and Banking

From security to customer services, artificial intelligence is changing the way banking is done. Artificial intelligence is a technology by which machines can learn from experience and perform the tasks that would previously require human intellect.

The use of technology has become prevalent in recently, and is most popular in banks. There are some finance companies that aid businesses with financial technology, including the technological innovation of payments and the automation of lending and borrowing. Banking and financial institutions are known for their personalized customer services, therefore everything is dependent on the customer service agents. These agents are responsible for various customer services such as phone calls, emails and websites. There are millions of calls per month through interactive voice response (IVR), distributed among agents and other operators in the present scenario. This is a huge task that requires significant human resources and manual work. To automate this traditional method of banks' customer services, Centurysoft introduced its AI technology-based customer response management. CRM solutions work as a smart solution for the banking sector and can handle thousands of instances without any human intervention with the vision of automating the system and cutting the cost of live agents. The CRM solutions will prove to be quick in achieving the desired targets. Centurysoft is the first company to introduce this AI-based solution, which is a unique multilingual system. Centurysoft promises to deliver 100% accuracy for speech and text recognition services. There are some other benefits provided by Centurysoft, which include that the banking policies and procedures can be fed to the system for error-free services for the customer. Banking-related queries might also have queries related to user account information such as recent transactions, and these and all other questions can be handled efficiently. The AI solution will act as a live agent to support bank customers and solve their queries. The system has been developed to save time, money and the related resources and to provide error-free quick responses.

7.1.4 Hurdles in Artificial Intelligence

Artificial intelligence is a technology that is going to impact the future of all countries. There are multiple use cases nowadays which are implemented on this technology. Still, this technology faces a number of hurdles and challenges that need to be resolved as soon as possible if we want the technology to reach its fullest potential [13].

1. **Lack of Computing Power**

   Artificial intelligence is all about working on data and machine learning and deep learning, which could require a considerable number of calculations and computations which have to be made very quickly. The processing power of the system has to be higher to do such significant estimation and calculations. The computing power we have nowadays will not manage the growing volume of data processing. Thus, the lack of computing power may slow down the computing and processing of continuously growing data.

2. **Lack of Knowledge**

   Over the last few years, artificial intelligence has been used in many companies and organization for developing new devices and the technology has been used in many different sectors. However, there are not enough people and organizations moving their businesses or ideas on to using artificial intelligence technology. One reason could be that there is a lack of people with knowledge of working on this technology and the related machines. Another possible reason could be the platforms and tools required to drive the AI work. Some organizations may be reluctant to choose and build the tools from scratch and prefer adopting tools and platforms from a ready-made solution to simply put the data into the device and get the result, while ignoring the technical operations inside the instrument.

3. **Trust Issues**

   Artificial intelligence is like a block box. Using the tools and platform for this technology does not provide information about what is happening inside. They may not understand how the decision is made, making them uncomfortable with using the technology. Since artificial intelligence works on multilayer neural networks, a person with little technical knowledge will not understand the predictions made by the system, which sometimes makes people uncomfortable with the technology, and building trust is not easy.

4. **Working on Similar Tracks**

   Implementing AI technology can be done either in a highly specialized manner or in a generalized way. A highly specialized AI can also be called applied AI, which is used to perform specific tasks, including giving a set of all the valid inputs to the system and getting the result measured until a highly effective output is received. Another form is generalized AI, which is implemented in robots where there is a predefined input to the system and predefined outputs, and the generalized AI doesn't vary too much.

7.1.5 Internet of Things (IoT)

The Internet of Things, or IoT, is influencing our lifestyle, in the form of how we react to our behavior. These devices vary from air conditioners that can be controlled with a smartphone of any user, to smart cars for providing the shortest routes, or a smartwatch that can be used for tracking the daily activity of a person. The IoT is a giant network with connected devices. These devices gather and share the data about how they are used and the environment in which they are operated. All this is done by the sensors embedded in every physical device, be it a mobile phone or an electrical appliance, bar code sensor, traffic lights, and almost everything that we come across in our day-to-day life. These sensors continuously emit data about the working state of the devices. The question may arise about how the sensors can share this massive amount of data and how the data can be put to good use. The IoT provides a common platform for all these devices to dump their data, and with a common language, all the devices are able to communicate with each other [14]. Data are emitted from various sources and sent to the IoT platform for security. The IoT platform integrates the collected data from multiple sources, other analytics are performed on the collected data, and the valuable information is extracted as per the requirement. Finally, the result is shared with other devices to improve the user experience and efficiency.

7.1.6 Healthcare Using the IoT

Healthcare is one of the most important areas of any society, with multiple problems being faced. Doctors find it difficult to visit rural areas and clinics frequently. Patients have to join long queues to obtain an appointment and treatment. Sometimes, for minor illnesses, there is no need for a physical check-up. Also, there may be no medical history available, either with the patient or with the clinic. With the use of the IoT, disease management can be improved. When the patient is monitored continuously, real-time health data are available; thus, the disease can be treated before it worsens [15]. The IoT could be beneficial in remote monitoring of patient health, statistics and diagnosis [16]. The IoT has made enabled diagnosis and medication to reach previously unreachable areas. Thus, the connected healthcare solutions and virtual infrastructures make the treatment precise and more effective. According to the "Alliance for Internet of Things Innovation (aioli. E.U.)" in its article on "Research and Innovation Priorities for IoT," the advanced automation and analytics of the IoT allows for more effective emergency support services. With this the patient receives a reminder to take their prescribed medicine and necessary actions to improve their health. The Internet has enabled the accurate collection of healthcare data, minimizing errors and making the medication as precise as possible.

7.1.7 Agriculture Using the IoT

We all know that agriculture has become a gamble, with the weather, water scarcity, soil fertility and pesticides being the major players. The IoT will be very beneficial for agriculture If we consider water management, an adequate water supply is essential for agriculture. An excess or shortage of water can kill crops. The IoT will make better water management possible when coupled with sensors, data and other machinery. This could be done with automated water sprinkling, which operates on the crop field on a timely basis, based on the type of crop, type of soil and weather conditions [17]. Weather forecasting and other dynamic data inputs can affect crop productivity significantly. This ensures accurate and efficient communication to farmers of real-time data related to agriculture, weather forecasts, soil quality, etc. With integrated IoT devices, pest control and management can prove a great help to farmers [18]. Observation, inspection, identification, record tracking and automated spraying of pesticides at the right time also are possible. The devices installed with the IoT are very useful in collecting real-time data and analyzing the data from every crop and their growth, thus making it easier for the farmer to predict the crop quality [19]. Other benefits of IoT in agriculture could include remote crop monitoring, making it easier for farmers to monitor their crops from any location and at any time, which could help them take the necessary action. Different crops require different weather conditions, and before the cultivation of any crop, the weather forecast could be conducive. IoT devices could play an essential role in climate monitoring for harvesting and also play a vital role in forecasting the weather conditions so that proper action could be taken to protect crops from damage [20].

7.1.8 IoT in Smart Cities

The IoT is transforming today's cities into the smarter cities of tomorrow. Some IoT systems will define the smart cities of tomorrow. With an IoT smart street light automation system, it will be easier for any town to save energy by monitoring street lighting as there would be a centralized control and reporting center which could obtain data from the IoT devices installed in the street lights, which would send data from the street lights of a particular area [21]. The IoT devices would be able to send fault reports and alerts if any street light was damaged or not working correctly. Thus, the complete information from all the areas in regard to maintenance work could be done quickly and in a single visit. IoT waste automation helps to ensure a clean environment. The installed IoT devices located throughout a city would help in improving cleanliness at a much lower fuel cost. IoT monitoring will also help to detect and predict water logging in any area enabling quick remedial action to be taken [22]. The smart cities could also have pollution monitoring and ensure a pollution-free city by monitoring the local air quality [23] and predicting geographical pollutants. Also, with gathering and analyzing data, adequate measures can be taken to curb pollution. Since the numbers of cars are increasing almost daily in most cities, there needs to be improved parking areas. The IoT could be helpful in automatic parking spot reservation, which would make the allocation more efficient, and space sharing could also enable hassle-free parking [24]. As discussed earlier, the IoT could help predict the weather conditions by monitoring the weather in different areas. Through accurate weather prediction, the city's citizens could plan their day more efficiently [25].

7.1.9 Challenges with the IoT

Humanity is moving toward a smart world. Products, service, methods and tools are all working toward technologies that will give benefits to society. The IoT is one such technology that is becoming increasingly popular. This technology is providing services to the community in tracking and analyzing data and resources. However, as with any new technology, there are always some associated challenges which may cause some organizations not to implement it in their business.

7.1.10 Security

IoT technology deals in data collection, and all data collection technology comes with security threats; these security threats can be hazardous, whether from a nation or a cyber-gang. Hackers attempt to find out and hack data that is sensitive and insecure. Therefore, applying security to sensitive data like healthcare data needs greater protection from various risks. Cloud computing could be one option to store the data collected by IoT devices. Cloud computing could protect data to some extent, but both cloud computing and the IoT are not easy for new users.

7.1.11 Integration

Integration of IoT devices with other systems is a challenge and may become complicated. Integration of the IoT includes IoT devices, data integration, back-end systems and sometimes third-party middleware. Therefore, implementation and integration of the IoT with another system may be extremely difficult. To deal with these complications, organizations have been using different methods to add sensors and cameras into the current technology and environment [26], which could be beneficial in collecting and analyzing the data collected to help in analyzing the machine performance.

7.1.12 Lack of Experience and Expertise

Employees working on IoT technology and related devices must have experience and expertise of working with these IoT devices to better integrate and implement devices with the system. However, the problem arises when organizations are unable to find a person with experience working with the IoT. Many employees have previous experience of working with the technology, but moving on to a new technology may require time to gain the relevant expertise.

7.1.13 Blockchain: Adding Value to a Business Process

Blockchain technology has seen remarkable growth recently, with the technology being used for a various purposes in addition to cryptocurrency. The technology is being used in multiple sectors, including education, healthcare and improving the quality of business processes. For many different companies, a matter of concern is the design, execution, monitoring and improvement of the business process. For this, many different companies are using multiple systems that support the execution of the process. A business company works on mutual trust with its customers and other business partners. Blockchain thus provides an environment where the interorganizational process can operate and execute in a trustworthy manner, without requiring the trust of a specific individual,, rather depending on the data in the blockchain. The blockchain network can provide end-to-end traceability, and real-time audits can be done using timestamps and digital signatures. Transactions that are an essential part of a business process can use the smart contracts of blockchain technology where the transactions are executed transparently to other participants in the blockchain network. Smart contracts are a small piece of code or small programs on a blockchain. Smart contracts run automatically whenever certain conditions are fulfilled. Thus, smart contracts can be used as an agreement between the blockchain network users to verify the transaction without the interference of a third party, and the rules once created cannot be changed or modified, which allows the business parties to work transparently.

Blockchain can benefit a business by tracing back the items or any product that it is trading. We know that it becomes challenging if the thing we are dealing with is lost or becomes untraceable. Blockchain thus comes into the picture as the complete information of the item with the exact date and time of the item being sent or received is recorded on the blockchain. There is no possibility that the data will get lost not be able to be recovered. However, every business needs to take precautions when investing in blockchain technology

[27] as it is not guaranteed that every company will benefit from a blockchain network in both design and process improvement, and any unorganized or unorderly structure that is implemented on blockchain may lead to strategic failures. Thus, companies must first determine which part of the business or which application needs to be inducted into the blockchain. Hence, from a business perspective the right approach at the right time may gain maximum benefit in a business process.

7.1.14 Retail Chain Industry

The retail chain industry is the one of most significant nowadays. Current retail clients are worried about getting fair trade and actual cases that retailers make about their stock [28]. Social media has encouraged the single-channel client to become conscious, well informed and product authenticated. This has caused retailers to improve the quality of the products they receives from the producer and so also the products they are selling to their customers. Furthermore, retailers stand to increase their operational favorable circumstances with these upgraded quality activities. Big e-commerce companies, like Amazon and Flipkart, have enabled easy access to their customers through door-to-door delivery. In 2018, the United States generated retail sales with a net worth of $5.3 trillion. The figure is still growing because retailers have upgraded them to new technologies, and consumers can now easily connect to retailers, be it physically or online. As the retail chain industry is growing so fast in this digital world, consumers are increasingly interested in buying products online. Sometimes the customer receives a wrong or fake product, thus it becomes necessary to bring the retail industry into a blockchain network.

7.1.15 Blockchain in the Retail Industry

Blockchain technology simplifies the relationship with the customer, reducing fraud and improving the speed of the supply chain. This technology enhances the rate of transactions and cash flow. Today, customers are provided with many choices of different products, and they demand the best outcome, coupled with reliability. Consumers are not satisfied with just the label of originality; they need a mechanism to track the product's authenticity. Blockchain provides such an environment and is the solution to this problem in the retail chain; for example, if a customer wants to buy diamond jewelry, the information regarding the jewelry can be stored on a blockchain tag. This tag will give the complete information regarding the source of origin of the diamond, details of the processing, date of manufacturing, etc., which provides the customer with a quality check of the diamond as the tags would be verified by the authorities responsible for the reviews as the data stored on the blockchain cannot be changed or modified as the blockchain

Simplicity   Reducing   Increased   Faster payment   Stronger
                fraud   speed   relationship

FIGURE 7.1
Blockchain in a retail chain.

provides the feature of immutability. Once the customer is satisfied with the quality and authenticity of the diamond, they can pay the retailer directly through smart contracts. All the information regarding the customers buying products and the transactions are stored on the blockchain. Customers can also check that no one uses their data held earlier on the blockchain network for any illegal activity such as buying products using their identity. Hence the blockchain can help in building trust between the consumer and retailers (see Figure 7.1).

In the retail supply chain, we have described the network of retailers and consumers. Next, we will see how the blockchain can be applied when the producer and the manufacturer enter the network.

7.1.16 Supply Chain Management

The supply chain industry is enormous and is going to grow over time. Supply chain management is a globally connected network of individuals; organizations deliver products and services starting from the raw materials from the supplier and giving the end product to customers. The supply chain involves the flow of information, products and cash. The supply chain involves three basic entities, a supplier, a producer or a manufacturer, and a customer [29] (see Figure 7.2). The basic flow between the three entities would be: a producer with the raw material sells it to the supplier, the supplier sells it to the manufacturer, which in turn again sells it to the supplier who sells the product to the retailer before reaching the customer as shown in Figure 7.9. Now the flow will start from the customer end as cash goes to the raw material producer via the supplier. All of the information is documented from the producer to the customer and the customer to the supplier. A problem with essential supply chain management is the timely delivery of the product. The product passes through various channels, so its timely delivery sometimes is an issue of concern. The central problem in the essential supply chain business is duplicity or counterfeit products in the market, whether this is a food supply chain, a pharmaceutical supply chain or a garment supply chain, etc. Blockchain technology can resolve the issues involved in the primary supply chain industry.

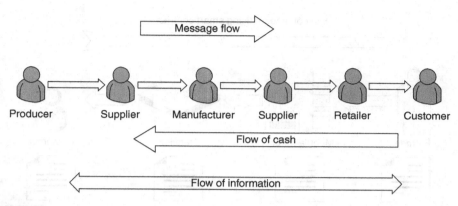

FIGURE 7.2
Basic supply chain management.

7.1.17 Blockchain for Supply Chain Management

Now that we have seen the problems associated with essential supply chain management, with blockchain technology, we can eliminate these problems of fake products, counterfeit medicines, maintaining the records of transactions, the trail from the middle man to every stage of the supply chain. These are some of the major problems in a supply chain.

Blockchain technology provides the necessary security in a tamper-proof and transparent manner when applied to essential supply chain management. With smart contracts, the transactions between parties can take place more securely and ensure privacy protection [30]. A blockchain technology works in a decentralized network and consists of a shared ledger. This shared ledger contains all the information of work done by all the parties in the network and is shared with all the parties of the network.

7.1.18 Blockchain in Food Supply Chain Management

When blockchain is applied in food supply management, it includes the farmer as the producer, producing the raw material and using his smartphone to directly put on the blockchain that the raw material is ready to be taken by the manufacturer, thus eliminating the need for a middleman who takes a commission from both the producer and manufacturer. The farmer can scan the code of the raw material and put it in the shared ledger of the blockchain, giving the complete details of the raw material, and maintaining transparency. The manufacturer has a system where it can send an alert to the farmer regarding the use of the raw material until the final product is available. The manufacturer can now make the transaction in blockchain with the smart contract to the raw material producer. Now the farmer has a much

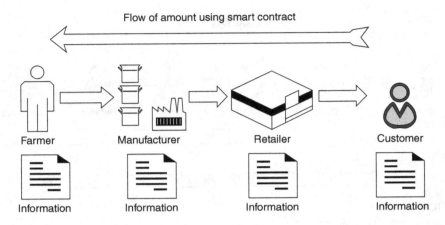

FIGURE 7.3
Food supply management in blockchain.

better record of the trade and knows when payment will be made for the raw material with some visibility in the supply chain. The manufacturer can further take the product from the raw material and send an alert to the retailer or the customer directly. All the transactions to all the parties will be done with the smart contract. Now, when the customer receives the end product, they can check with the shared ledger, the producer, the manufacturer and all other information shared by the producer and manufacturer (see Figure 7.3).

7.1.19 Pharmaceuticals Supply Chain

According to Rodrigo Couto de Souza [31], the counterfeit medicines business is worth around U.S. \$200 million. The WHO estimated around 120,000 people die in Africa every year due to fake drugs for malaria. The global counterfeit medicine trade is also operated by a transactional criminal network that supports worldwide business and technology infrastructure, and there is no record of tracing these fake medicines. This problem of counterfeit medicine is not limited to developing countries but also developed countries. The actual pharmaceutical supply chain model in Figure 7.4 involves various entities such as distribution channel, retailer, manufacturer and customer, so it looks very complex in structure as there are many steps involved. For a manufacturing company, there is a lot of information to be recorded such as details of the material provider, licensing for the manufacturer, demand from retailers and manufacturing orders. The problem with the current pharma supply chain management includes the electronic interoperability system for tracking and tracing all drugs through the supply chain, which requires many parameters to be recorded, such as transaction history, transaction information, transaction number, etc.

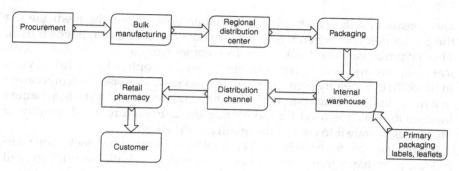

FIGURE 7.4

Pharmaceuticals supply chain.

Another problem is storing data of all the transactions and the possibility of losing this data in the event of a disaster. These problems create a lot of problems in the essential supply chain management of the pharmaceuticals industry. Thus, there was a need for a technology to give greater security and transparency to the pharmaceuticals industry.

Blockchain is one such technology that came in being about a decade ago. This technology is being used in various industry sectors, from agriculture to finance and supply chain management, and the pharmaceutical industry is one such part of supply chain management that is using blockchain technology.

Of the different types of blockchain, a permission type of blockchain would be most helpful in the pharmaceutical industry.

Critical elements of blockchain such as hash functions, smart contracts, the IoT and interoperability play an essential role when applied to any network. With the help of blockchain technology, each company can now maintain its data secured with cryptographic algorithms such as hash functions that make sure only the intended party can use the data. The blockchain network is a decentralized type of network which prevents the loss of data. Every transaction made between every party involved in the medicines supply chain can use smart contracts as a medium for trades. A smart contract is a program code that executes on its own when used by network users. The smart contract makes sure that the transactions made are only to the intended recipient. It also provides transparency between the users of the technology. This element of the blockchain will eliminate the requirement for the middleman, which was essential previously in the pharmaceutical supply chain.

The biggest problem in the primary pharmaceutical supply chain was counterfeit medicine being supplied to retailers. With blockchain technology, this problem can also be removed using another element: the Internet of Things (IoT). IoT devices can help track medicines from the manufacturer or producer to the consumer. With IoT devices in place, the manufacturer and consumer will get complete information about when the medicine left the production unit, when it reached the consumer and through which path. The consumer can also track if the drug comes from a trusted pharmaceutical company and is not fake. Another important application of IoT devices in blockchain is quality control, where IoT devices can sense the temperature of a medicine and drugs parcel. Sadhukhan [32] developed a start-up named modum.io, which is used for monitoring the temperature and humidity of medicines in transit to control the quality of the drugs.

Pharma companies have been very slow in implementing blockchain technology, as implementing the technology is costly. Still, this technology will undoubtedly help the industry in many ways if implemented.

7.1.20 Blockchain in the Business Travel Industry

Whenever a person thinks of traveling on a family vacation or business trip, which are the most frequent types of trips, they look for a travel agent or tour operator. A tour operator plans the complete itineraries for the traveler from the flight to traveling to the hotel and further traveling on-site, including providing meals. The traveler relies on the travel operator and travel agents for convenience for their trip (see Figure 7.5).

When a person is going on a business trip, there is some risk involved with the passenger name record (PNR). The traveler has no idea how much data are connected with the PNR code, and lots of personal information can be obtained from the PNR if it falls into the wrong hands. Consider a situation where a traveler forgets their boarding pass for a plane; the information such as itinerary and identity could be taken from the information printed on the

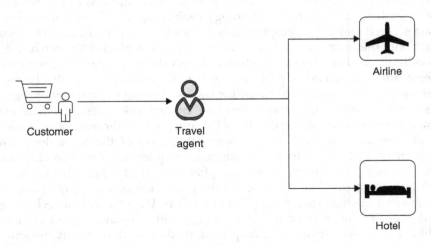

FIGURE 7.5
Basic travel industry.

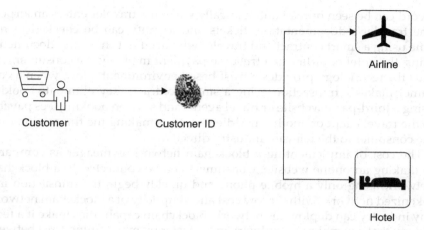

FIGURE 7.6
Travel industry with blockchain.

boarding pass. In the worst-case situation, a hacker can log into a frequent flyer's account and get passport information and other confidential data.

Blockchain technology has come up with a lot of security and privacy solutions to resolve the insecurities associated with the old PNR systems. A blockchain network works on a series of ledgers or block, with each block containing different information. The digital ledgers can only be accessed and viewed by the parties with the unique code but they cannot modify the contents of the digital catalogue. This unique code would be helpful for travel agents and travel management companies, providing greater confidence as they would be able to have more control over unforeseen circumstances and be able to arrange different transport, convenience, privacy, payment and security groundworks. Blockchain technology has simplified the identification process and increased the security level. With blockchain technology in use by the travel business, the travel agency/agents can now track the travelers' identity in different places and ensure data security(see Figure 7.6). If blockchain technology was used in the travel tourism business, travelers would not need to show their passport at varying stages of the journey. Instead, the traveler information could be stored on the blockchain network and transmitted automatically in advance, which would speed up the process. The traveler's data could also be used by the travel agents and the respective travel companies using unique codes. They could gain to the access controls so that the traveler receives timely authentication during the whole journey.

Another implementation of blockchain technology in the travel business could eliminate the middleman from the network. With blockchain technology, a consumer can directly book a ticket with a hotel or an airline using a smart contract. A smart contract can be programmed so that the traveler's record can be seen or read automatically when the traveler enters an airport. The traveler's documentation, tickets and identity can be checked in real time using a smart contract and traveler who need not show any documents. Thus, the hotel or airline can trust the payment made by the consumer, and thus the technology provides a trust-based environment. Now, when a consumer makes a transaction using a smart contract, they eliminate booking using a third-party website or travel agents and save on booking fees payable to the travel agent or another middleman, thus making the transaction from the consumer to the relevant industry directly.

The cost of implementing a blockchain network is meager as compared to making an online website. Consumers can be connected to a blockchain network using only a mobile phone and quickly begin the transaction in a tokenized network. With the low cost and simplicity of a blockchain network, any industry can deploy this network. Blockchain capabilities make it a technology that can make any industry grow faster by maintaining trust between two parties. The travel industry is one such industry that has just begun to adopt this new technology. Changing from an existing platform to a new platform may take some time, but use of this latest technology will benefit the industry.

7.1.21 Blockchain in the Hospitality Business

As we have already discussed about the blockchain in a travel business, when people travel to a destination, be it for business or a vacation, the hospitality industry serves many of these people. The hospitality industry has also entered this technical phase of operation (see Figure 7.7). The way consumers access the services of the hospitality industry and pay for the same, such as through the Internet, has completely changed. Also, the middleman/

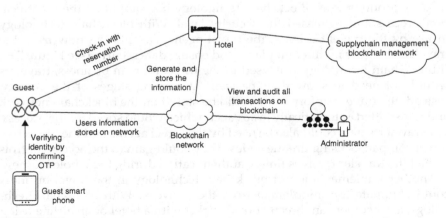

FIGURE 7.7
Blockchain in the hospitality business.

agents are making profits through booking and cancellations. According to one website, scalablockchain.com, the hotel industry was expected to generate around 500 billion U.S. dollars in revenue in 2016. This shows how big the hotel industry is. One of the major challenges this industry is facing is customer retention. It sometimes is difficult to meet the high expectations of customers at discounted prices. Different websites are coming into the market, with each one giving the best price that will benefit the middleman and the customer, but not the hotel. Hence the expectations of the customers are always increasing in respect to getting the best service for the money paid, which is not possible for all hotels while also giving a cut to agents and middlemen, thus they fall short in this sector.

Blockchain technology is gaining popularity in the hospitality sector also. Most other sectors are already using this technology and gaining the benefits of blockchain technology. Hotels and their suppliers need to update the content with the latest information constantly, such as new facilities provided with pictures and videos for the customers on their websites. A blockchain network could provide such a facility by providing a single location where all hotels need to update their information by registering themselves and storing their updated content on the blockchain network. A blockchain network could be very helpful for making payments easier. Payments are a crucial part of the hospitality industry, and blockchain provides a network where the payments and transactions can be made in a more secure manner. Cryptocurrencies can be used for making the payments and to settle any outstanding sums. This could reduce the costs incurred by the old methods of settling finance such as payments by credit cards or bank transfer. Parties involved in the transaction must be eager to obtain and utilize the pertinent cryptocurrencies which may be a barrier until the cryptocurrencies are more widely used.

A smart contract is a new way of transferring funds to second parties. A smart contract is program code which executes automatically. A smart contract can be used to send the funds for making payments to hotels against the deposit and for cancellation fees. The automatic execution of a smart contract can speed up the transaction process being transferred among the parties and save time and work related with the collection and processing of payments. When blockchain cryptocurrency is used for payment settlement instead of credit cards, the credit card fee incurred during the transaction can be eliminated. There are some cases reported of credit card fraud, which has been very high in recent years. According to a Nilson report in 2016, the worldwide credit card fraud losses were estimated to be around $24.71 billion. Now, when a funds transaction is completed with smart contracts the transaction is done using cryptocurrencies, and credit card fraud will also be reduced.

With the blockchain technology entering the hospitality industry customers can now directly book a taxi when booking a hotel. All the facilities in addition to the hotel booking can be made directly to the supplier, eliminating the intermediaries. This process can also reduce dependence on a middleman.

A blockchain network could be useful for tracking a guest from leaving their home for the airport to the time they check-in for the flight and even reaching the hotel. This tracking information would increase the effectiveness by reducing the wait time during the check-in process at the airport and thus increase customer satisfaction and thereby increase customer retention. When customers are also present in the blockchain network they have the right to allow the hotel and other parties in the network to access their information. The guest also gets information on who is viewing their data. Hence blockchain technology has the capability to give flawlessly incorporated guest services without encroaching into the visitor's privacy.

In the hospitality industry food is another product that customers pay for and, when the food served is not of a good enough quality, the customers have negative attitudes about the hotel. Hence, tracking and monitoring of food items is another major concern. With the blockchain the supply chain management can be extended to hotels and restaurants to provide better food in terms of quality and safety. The hotel industry should collaborate with food suppliers, and the food suppliers should also be added into the blockchain network with customers and other parties so that the customers can also enquire into and see the origin and quality of the food being served. Thus, the hotel and restaurant can build trust with their customers regarding the quality and safety of the food served.

7.1.22 Challenges with Implementing Blockchain

Blockchain technology has great potential to be included in business processes and benefit business process management innovatively. A blockchain-based network can be a secure network that provides complete privacy to the network, but companies need to generate revenue at the end of the day. Therefore, from an individual organization's perspective, there are some challenges to the adoption of this technology. This technology is still in its early stage, and there are some limitations and confusion around specific areas such as system performance, scalability, cost, etc., therefore there is a need to understand the business goals and try to align them with the choice of technology. For example, a public, private or consortium type of blockchain could be used and the type of consensus mechanism to be used will also have a profound impact on the business of an organization. The most significant challenges with the adoption of blockchain technology will be industry standards, but what is encouraging is that many industries are using or shortly plan to move to this decentralized, immutable technology.

The problem with adopting blockchain technology is moving the existing system from one technology to another different technology. Any industry working on a platform and suddenly moving to another platform can be challenging for any industry.

Another challenge could be inconsistency with the technology partner. Some partners are somewhat more front-footed and ready to invest their money, time and resources into blockchain technology. In contrast, some participants are more distracted by other considerations or resources. There could be an issue in implementing blockchain technology as the technology deployed may be legal in one country and not permitted in another, which could be a problem in interorganization businesses, so the technology has to global.

Scalability is one of the most significant concerns about blockchain technology when the payment application is discussed. According to www.networkcomputing.com, a visa process may take up to 1667 transactions per second, whereas Bitcoin takes three to four and Ethereum handles about 15 transactions per second. The issue of scalability may decrease the speed of transactions and might affect directly or indirectly the business process and the parties involved in the blockchain network.

A lack of knowledge regarding blockchain technology is another concern. A blockchain network for food supply chain management includes the producer to a customer, who might not have sufficient knowledge of working on the technology, which would be a monumental task to overcome.

7.2 Revolutionary Impact of Spectrum Computing, Brain Wave Mechanism and Smart Contract in the Digital World

7.2.1 Spectrum Computing in the Digital World

Today, no matter the type of industry, they are speeding toward the outcome, which is critical for their mission. They are doing it with the flexibility to meet demands whatever the workload would be while minimizing the cost [33]. IBM spectrum computing is a technology that focuses on these issues. At the heart of the solution is the cluster virtualization software. This type of software is commonly used in high-performance computing and it is gaining use in data analytics. New-generation applications and frameworks like big data, artificial intelligence and containers do not run on a single system. They run on 10s, 100s and 1000s of systems comprised of a computing cluster. Therefore, for this, the user needs software that automatically optimizes a computing cluster which provides faster results, and is easier to manage and easier to scale for multiple operations. With the IBM spectrum computing, users can share a group to many users across the lines of a business while running multiple applications simultaneously and on the same infrastructure. This might include different versions of an application, for example, numerous instances of sparc or Hadoop. Cluster virtualization also enables the consolidation of multiple clusters. This increases the neutralization to deliver better performance of the group. At the spectrum computing core is an intelligent scheduler that runs the right workload with the right resources at the right time, optimizing on-premises cloud and hybrid resources to deliver better service and provide the IT staff with the flexibility to meet the new and changing needs in the spectrum computing. The priority workloads are handled by suspending the lower priority workloads, then resuming the lower priority workloads after the high-priority workload is complete. With spectrum computing, the clusters are always available. If a server fails, critical services and workload are automatically restarted on different servers. With the interfaces available, users are able to access and use the clusters. This allows the user to focus on the outcomes. In spectrum computing, the comprehensive monitoring, reporting and administration tools allow IT staff to manage numerous systems from a single interface. Spectrum computing also helps to maximize the current IT investments by supporting a genius architecture like power, X86, GPUs, Linux and Windows. The integration of spectrum computing with the latest technologies includes opensource framework like the docker, OpenPower, for big data (Hadoop) and containers (SPARC), that will support the future growth. IBM's spectrum computing has a solid and robust record of success. Some of the most demanding workloads also run on IBM's spectrum computing with shared computer clusters for over two decades. The users of spectrum computing get faster results with minimal downtime and at a very low cost (see Figure 7.8).

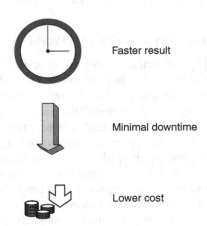

FIGURE 7.8
Spectrum computing.

7.2.2 Brain Wave Mechanism in the Digital World

A brain wave is the electrical voltage that oscillates in the brain, and measures a few millionths of a volt [34]. When a person is in a deep sleep or watching a video or maybe taking an exam, the human brain is abuzz with that activity. There are millions of electrical pulses passing between the neurons that are sending messages to each other. Now, when those signals spread, clusters of neurons start getting feedback from the other neurons and a network of cells to synchronize their firing. However, it becomes a repeating cycle or a brainwave or, according to neuroscientists, also called oscillations. That organized electrical activity is strong enough to be detected by electrodes on the scalp with a technique called electroencephalography (EEG). EEG allows brainwaves to be studied to try to make sense of the brain. The brainwaves can be linked to things like consciousness, memory, and maybe even specific diseases. There are many different electrical patterns, defined by their frequency. They are measured in cycles or the number of times the neurons are firing per second. Brainwaves also vary in amplitude, with lower amplitudes as they speed up. There are five mains types, and there are no hard and fast rules about their functions, but generally, the higher the frequency of the wave [35], the more alert and awake the person is. The slowest of these five waves, which are relatively high amplitude, are *delta waves*. The delta waves are typically linked with deep sleep. Slightly faster than delta waves are *theta waves*. Theta waves are often associated with day-dreaming, being deeply relaxed or meditating. After theta waves are *alpha waves*, which are common when the person is awake but very relaxed, such as when the person is sitting with their eyes closed. *Beta waves* are even higher in frequency and lower in amplitude and seem to happen when the person is awake but thinking about something. The smallest, fastest oscillations are *gamma waves*. These tend to occur when the person is intensely focused on something. Whichever position or activity the person is involved with, the reality is that the human brain is abuzz with all different frequency waves. However, any particular brainwave is very dominant at any specific moment, depending upon what the person is doing and how the person feels at that particular point in time. Let us suppose a person is sitting in the park and lots of alpha and theta waves are present, there will still be some beta waves that might be going on in the background. The brain does not have the same frequencies throughout an whole episode.

The five types of brain waves recognized are described in Table 7.1.

From the individual reading obtained on an EEG, it has been observed that different brain regions are more commonly linked with certain waves. Alpha waves, for instance, are usually the strongest at the back of the brain in the occipital lobe, which handles a person's vision. One of the fantastic things with brain waves is that these expected frequencies are remarkably similar across different species such as cats, bats and humans [36]. However, at the same time, they can be very different between individuals. Some

TABLE 7.1

Types of Brain Waves

Frequency Band	Frequency	Brain States
Gamma (γ)	35 Hz	Concentration
Beta (β)	12–35 Hz	Anxiety dominant, active, external attention, relaxed
Alpha (α)	8–12 Hz	Very relaxed, passive attention
Theta (θ)	4–8 Hz	Deeply relaxed, inward focused
Delta (δ)	0.5–4 Hz	Sleep

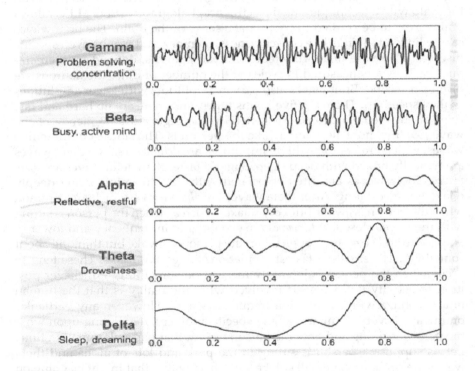

FIGURE 7.9

Brain wave samples for different waveforms.
Source: [35].

neuroscientists have even proposed that a snapshot of all the brain waves could be used to identify a person, like a fingerprint. Therefore, in some way, measuring brainwaves could be very powerful. Brainwaves punctuated with spikes can give signs of a seizure. Recent works have even suggested the use of different brainwaves to help us to learn. According to research, beta waves might reinforce neural connections to improve memory [37]. At the same time, theta waves are a way of saying to the brain that you have forgotten something. Gamma waves are exciting to neurobiologists, too, as people with Alzheimer's disease don't seem to use them as much as other people. However, in an experiment in mice, restoring gamma waves reduced beta-amyloid, the plaque protein associated with the disease.

7.2.3   Smart Contract in the Digital World

One of the key technology innovations of second-generation blockchains has been developing what are called smart contracts. A smart contract is a computer code stored inside a blockchain that includes the contractual agreements. Smart contracts are a self-executable code that comes with the terms of agreement or operation directly written in two lines of code stored and executed on a blockchain computer [38]. In a traditional sense, a contract is a binding agreement between two or more parties to do or not do something. Each party involved must trust the other parties to fill their side of the obligation. They are a written or spoken agreement that is intended to be enforced by law. An assortment of additional contractual agreements forms the institutional foundations of our modern society and economy, which have evolved since ancient times. The economy of any country is a massive set of contractual agreements that are currently created and enforced by a centralized authority, such as insurance companies and banks, which are again supported by the higher centralized authority in the system. Our society and economies are entirely dependent upon third-party organizations to maintain and enforce those contractual agreements. Smart contracts feature these kinds of deals to act or not act, but they remove the need for the trusted third party between the members involved in the arrangements. This is because a smart contract is defined by the computer code and executed or enforced by the code itself automatically without discretion at such blockchains. Innovative contract technology can remove reliance on the centralized system and enable people to create contractual agreements that can be automatically enforced and executed by a computer code. These smart contacts are decentralized in that they do not exist on a single centralized server but are distributed and self-executing across a network of nodes. This means that an untrusted third party can transact with each other in a much more fluid fashion without depending upon the third parties to initiate and maintain the transaction rules.

Likewise, the smart contract enables autonomy between members that means that after it is launched and running an agreement in its initiating, agents need not be in further contracts. One example of this situation is one in which four people are pooling their money to invest in something that will return interest to them. A smart contract could be programmed on the blockchain to take any claim created divided into four and send each amount to the corresponding wallets of the different stakeholders. A smart contract is then really just an account on the blockchain controlled by the code instead of the user because it is on the blockchain; it is immutable, which means there is no possibility of changing the code. Thus, the investor is assured that they will get their fair share automatically. The code will dictate how the process takes place, and no individual has the power to change the code, be it an organization, government or censor. Nothing can alter or manipulate the smart contract code. In this sense, it is said that *code is law* in the sense that code will definitely execute no matter what. As an example, a logistic company could use a smart contract to run the code. If I receive cash on delivery at this particular location, then it triggers a supplier request to stock a new item since the existing article has just been delivered.

A combination of smart contract with a smart contract-encoded property will give an idea of intellectual property [39]. Bright property is property whose ownership is controlled through blockchain-encoded contractual agreements. For example, a pre-established smart contract could automatically transfer the right of a vehicle title from the holding company to the individual owner when all the loan instalments have been cleared. The key idea of the smart property is controlling the ownership and access to an asset by having it registered as a digital asset on the ledger and connecting that to a smart contract. In some cases, the physical world hard assets could quite literally be controlled through the blockchain.

Like all the algorithms, any smart contract would require an input value and can only act if certain predefined conditions are met. When a particular deal is reached, the smart contract changes its state and executes programmatically predefined algorithms, automatically triggering an event on the blockchain. Thus, the working of the overall contracts can only be as good as the inputted data. If both the data are inputted into the system, then the system might give false results. Blockchain cannot access its data outside its network, thus requiring some form of trusted data feed as input to the system, called an *oracle* [40]. An oracle is a data feed provided by an external service designed for smart contracts on the blockchain. Oracle provide the external data and triggers the smart contract executions when some predefined conditions are met. Such a condition could be any data like weather temperature or quantity of items in stock. An oracle in the blockchain and smart contract context is then an agent that finds and verifies real-world occurrences and provides this information to the blockchain network that the smart contract can use. However, an oracle is a third-party service that is not part of the blockchain consensus mechanism. Thus, whether it is a newsfeed website or a sensor, the source of information needs to be trustworthy.

There are countless advantages to a smart contract. First, the smart contract is automatic, and so it can remove the time and cost associated with managing and enforcing them, making them more efficient as they are cheaper and faster to run. Through this form of automation, a much more significant amount of exchanges could take place that otherwise would never have happened. In this way, we can see how the distributed ledgers and smart contracts are a crucial part in enabling a genuine service to the economy where the temporal usage displaces the ownership through the on-demand provisioning of services.

Second, the smart contract could be beneficial in reducing corruption any in the world [41]. Since smart contracts are a transparent program code in their working and automatic execution, this leaves little room for an organization or individual to modify it according to their advantage.

Third, they reduce the dependency upon a centralized organization as people can set up their contractual agreements peer to peer. Thus, limiting the arbitrary power of centralized organizations.

Last, a smart contract can also deliver certainty as they guarantee a specific set of predetermined outcomes, enabling all parties to know exactly what will happen.

There are also some limitations associated with smart contracts. By automating the execution of a contract, they are dependent upon formal rules with well-specified inputs and leave very little room for an assortment of eventualities which laws may need to be slightly altered because of unforeseen circumstances. Many unpredictable and unexpected events in the real world could occur, and rules sometimes need to be flexible and adaptable to accommodate this fact. This is one advantage of having human oversight as people are much more capable of judging such circumstances and responding appropriately to complex unforeseen eventualities. Hence, the degree to which the smart contract is relative to the kind of environment operated in more complex situations, will often need a governing body to intervene when needed. This creates new complications surrounding governance that are yet to be figured out.

References

1. Anand Nayyar, V. P. (2016). Smart farming: IoT based smart sensors agriculture stick for live temperature and moisture monitoring using Arduino, cloud computing & solar technology. *The International Conference on Communication and Computing Systems (ICCCS-2016)*.

2. Archana Chougule, V. K. (2016). Using IoT for integrated pest management. *International Conference on Internet of Things and Applications (IOTA-2016)*.

3. Bruce, Hartley (2012). *The Internet of Things—Weather Monitoring Too*. Wellington: WMO.

4. Buzsáki, G. (2006). *Rhythms of the Brain*. Oxford University Press.

5. Abhang, Priyanka A., Bharti W. Gawali, and Suresh C. Mehrotra (2016). Technological Basics of EEG Recording and Operation of Apparatus.

In Introduction to EEG- and Speech-Based Emotion Recognition, pp. 19–50. Acadamic Press.

6. Center, M. N. (November 7, 2017). *Digital Agriculture: Farmers in India Are Using AI to Increase Crop Yields.* Available at: https://news.microsoft.com/; https://news.microsoft.com/en-in/features/ai-agriculture-icrisat-upl-india/; https://news.microsoft.com/en-in/features/ai-agriculture-icrisat-upl-india/

7. Chattopadhyay, P. S. (n.d.). *Digital Circuits.* Available at: https://nptel.ac.in/; https://nptel.ac.in/content/storage2/nptel_data3/html/mhrd/ict/text/108105113/lec1.pdf

8. Cristian Toma, A. A. (2019). IoT solution for smart cities' *pollution monitoring and the security challenges. Sensors,* 19(15), 3401.

9. David Gil, A. F.-M. (2016). Internet of Things: A review of surveys based on context aware intelligent services. *Sensors (Basel), 16,* 1069.

10. DeVries, P. D. (September 2016). An Analysis of cryptocurrency, bitcoin, and the future. *International Journal of Business Management and Commerce,* 1(2), 1–9.

11. Dino Quintero, D. d. (2017). *IBM Spectrum Computing Solutions.* Redbooks.

12. Divya, S. I. V. (2018). A self-diagnosis medical chatbot using artificial intelligence. *Journal of Web Development and Web Designing,* 3, 1–7.

13. Dr. Ovidiu Vermesan, D. P. (2013). *Internet of Things: Converging Technologies for Smart Environments and Integrated Ecosystems.* Aalborg, Denmark, River Publishers.

14. Evans, R. S. (2016). Electronic health records: Then, *now, and in the future. Yearb Med Inform.,* suppl. 1, 48–61.

15. Filippo Pesapane, M. C. (2018). Artificial intelligence in medical imaging: threat or opportunity? Radiologists again at the forefront of innovation in medicine. *European Radiology Experimental,* 2, 35.

16. Geetanjali Katare, G. (2015). Challenges in the Integration of Artificial Intelligence and Internet of Things. *International Journal of System and Software Engineering,* 6(15), 10–15.

17. Gurría, A. (2019). *Artificial Intelligence in Society.* Available at: https://ec.eur opa.eu/; https://ec.europa.eu/jrc/communities/sites/jrccties/files/eedfe e77-en.pdf

18. Himadri Nath Saha, S. A. (2017). Health monitoring using Internet of Things (IoT). *Industrial Automation and Electromechanical Engineering Conference (IEMECON).* Bangkok, Thailand: IEEE.

19. Hooper, M. (February 22, 2018). Available at: www.ibm.com/blogs/blockch ain/2018/02/top-five-blockchain-benefits-transforming-your-industry/; www.ibm.com

20. Ioannis Karamitsos, M. P. (2018). Design of the blockchain smart contract: A use case for real estate. *Journal of Information Security,* 9, 177–190.

21. Joshi, H. (November 2017). *Security and Privacy in the Digital World.* Available at: www2.deloitte.com/; www2.deloitte.com/content/dam/Deloitte/tr/Documents/risk/security-and-privacy-noexp.pdf

22. Brunnermeier, Markus K., James, Harold and Jean-Pierre Landau (2019). *The Digitalization of Money,* pp. 1–31. Working Papers.

23. Marr, B. (July 13, 2017). *The Biggest Challenges Facing Artificial Intelligence (AI) in Business and Society*. Available at: www.forbes.com/; www.forbes.com/sites/bernardmarr/2017/07/13/the-biggest-challenges-facing-artificial-intelligence-ai-in-business-and-society/#1fa9ad562aec
24. Nagothu, S. (2016). Weather based Smart watering system using soil sensor and GSM. *World Conference on Futuristic Trends in Research and Innovation for Social Welfare (Startup Conclave)*.
25. Panpatte, D. (October 2018). *Artificial Intelligence in Agriculture: An Emerging Era of Research*. Intutional Science, Vancouver, Canada.
26. Parkash Tambare, P. V. (2016). Internet of Things based intelligent street lighting system for smart city. *International Journal of Innovative Research in Science, Engineering and Technology*, 5, 7684–7691.
27. Perumal, T. (2015). Internet of Things (IoT) enabled water monitoring system. *IEEE 4th Global Conference on Consumer Electronics (GCCE). Osaka: IEEE*.
28. Priyanka A. Abhang, Bharti Gawali, and Suresh Mehrotra (2016). *Introduction to EEG- and Speech-Based Emotion Recognition*. ScienceDirect.
29. R. Suresh, B. P. (2018). IoT based weather monitoring system. IoT Based Weather Monitoring System.
30. Rashida Peete, K. M. (2019). Artificial intelligence in healthcare. In *Artificial Intelligence and Machine Learning for Business for Non-Engineers*, 233–259. CRC Press.
31. Rodrigo Couto de Souza, E. M. (2018). *The Uses of the Blockchain Smart Contracts to Reduce the Levels of Corruption*: Some Preliminary Thoughts. ACM Digital Library.
32. Sadhukhan, P. (2017). An IoT-based e-parking system for smart cities. *Sixth International Conference on Advances in Computing, Communications and Informatics (ICACCI '17)*.
33. Stephanie Baker, W. Xiang and I. Atkinson (November 2017). Internet of Things for Smart Healthcare: Technologies, Challenges, and Opportunities, *IEEE Access 5*, 26521–26544 .
34. Stuart D. Levi and Alex B. Lipton, S. A. (May 26, 2018). *An Introduction to Smart Contracts and Their Potential and Inherent Limitations*. Available at: corpgov.law.harvard.edu; https://corpgov.law.harvard.edu/2018/05/26/an-introduction-to-smart-contracts-and-their-potential-and-inherent-limitations/
35. Tasnim Makada, D. O. (2016). *Enhancing Memory Retention by Increasing Alpha and Decreasing Beta Brainwaves Using Music*. ACM Digital Library.
36. Voshmgir, S. (2019). Blockchain oracles. In Shermin Voshmgir, *Token Economy: How the Web3 reinvents the Internet*, 257. Token Kitchen, Berlin.
37. Makada, T., Ozair, D., Mohammed, M., & Abellanoza, C. (2016, June). Enhancing memory retention by increasing alpha and decreasing beta brainwaves using music. In *Proceedings of the 9th ACM international conference on pervasive technologies related to assistive environments* (pp. 1–4).
38. Levi, S. D., & Lipton, A. B. (2018, May). An introduction to smart contracts and their potential and inherent limitations. In *Harvard Law School Forum on Corporate Governance* (Vol. 10).
39. Karamitsos, I., Papadaki, M., & Al Barghuthi, N. B. (2018). Design of the blockchain smart contract: A use case for real estate. *Journal of Information Security*, 9(03), 177.

40. Voshmgir, S. (2020). *Token economy: How the Web3 reinvents the internet* (Vol. 2). Token Kitchen.

41. de Souza, R. C., Luciano, E. M., & Wiedenhöft, G. C. (2018, May). The uses of the Blockchain Smart Contracts to reduce the levels of corruption: Some preliminary thoughts. In *Proceedings of the 19th Annual International Conference on Digital Government Research: Governance in the Data Age* (pp. 1–2).

8

Conclusion

As this book discusses the convergence of blockchain, the IoT, and artificial intelligence, it will be a useful handbook for upgrading of readers' knowledge, which will enhance a new thought process of interdependent components into a common aspect. The digital platforms are the most changing platforms in the current era, and so their advancement in any platform will affect the whole process. The IoT mechanism has faced problems of security and privacy concerns as it converges with blockchain technology, however the pitfalls have become advantages in the various applications. The first chapter gaves an overview of the three technologies, blockchain, the IoT, and artificial intelligence with their fundamental aspects described. The following chapters explained the transformation of these mechanism in correlation with each other, While the final chapters discussed the futuristic approaches of these technologies with some examples (Figure 8.1).

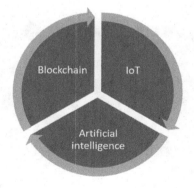

FIGURE 8.1
Convergence of blockchain, the IoT, and artificial intelligence.

DOI: 10.1201/9781003046462-9

Index

Note: Page numbers in **bold** refer to tables and those in *italic* refer to figures.

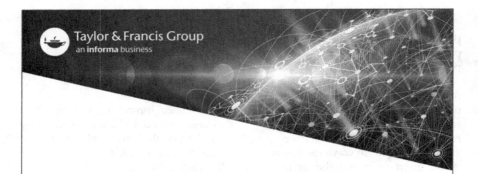

Printed in the United States
by Baker & Taylor Publisher Services